THIS HOLLER IS MY HOME

THIS HOLLER IS MY HOME

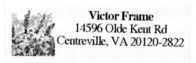

by Alyce Faye Bragg

Mountain State Press
Charleston, West Virginia

Some essays have been published in the weekday morning or Sunday editions of *The Charleston Gazette*, Charleston, West Virginia, *The Clay Herald*, Clay, West Virginia, or *The Clay Free Press*, Clay, West Virginia between October 28, 1981 and July 10, 1992.

International Standard Book Number: 0-941092-26-7

Library of Congress Catalog Card number: 92-062997

Mountain State Press
c/o The University of Charleston
2300 MacCorkle Avenue, S.E.
Charleston, WV 25304

Printed in the United States of America

This is a Mountain State Press book produced in affiliation with the University of Charleston, Charleston, West Virginia. Mountain State Press is solely responsible for editorial decisions.

Dedicated to the
memory of Alen Wayne Coon

Table of Contents

PROLOGUE

Nestled in the foothills of the sheltering Allegheny Mountains, there is a ragged, run-down patch of land that passes for a hillside farm. Located near the head of the holler (hollows in Appalachia are called "hollers") right before the winding country road leaves the creek and takes up the hill, it consists mostly of overgrown meadows, a few shaggy patches of timber, and fields of broomsage.

It could be any one of hundreds of hardscrabble farms that dot the hills in Clay County, and the same kind of country road crisscrosses much of West Virginia. This particular dirt road follows the meandering creek, crossing over it in several places with flat, wooden bridges. Here and there it hugs the hillside, while the lower bank breaks away in a sheer drop to the creek, revealing gray outcroppings of rock with scrubby pines clinging tenaciously to its sides. From the mouth of the holler, to the head of the creek, it couldn't be more than three or four miles, yet a whole lifetime can be lived here. This holler is my home.

The farm itself is little more than patches of poor soil flung helter skelter on rocky hillsides, and during its heyday probably didn't produce more than three or four acres of corn. It may have supported a dozen head of cattle, and a work horse or two. Why anyone would choose to live out their allotted days here, instead of moving on to greener pastures, is a mystery to many people.

The winters here are often harsh and cold, and deep poverty is all too evident. Yet I have known people who have lived their entire lives up one of these hollers, raised families, and died without journeying more than ten miles from their birthplace.

I remember one young man from my childhood, who grew up here in the hills and had not traveled any farther than the county seat of Clay — about an eight mile distance. One day he boarded the Greyhound bus and traveled to Charleston. After a day of stunned sightseeing, he climbed aboard the bus and told the driver, "Let me off at the mouth of the holler." When the bewildered bus driver asked where on earth that was, the young man gave him a look of withering scorn, "Man, everybody knows where the mouth of the holler is!"

It is not because we don't know any other way of life that we stay here. We have traveled to other places and visited beautiful states. We have toured the south where the Spanish moss waves graceful tendrils in the warm air. We have seen roses blooming at Christmas, and exotic flowers and bushes. We viewed the bayous of Louisiana and watched the ceaseless waves beat upon miles of sandy beaches. We walked the beaches of Delaware, where the beautiful white sand sparkles in the sunshine. Yet, how glad we were to get home again. Our eyes grew weary of looking at the flat landscape, and our friendly hills seemed to enclose us in a warm embrace. The brooks and woods seemed to murmur, "Walk with us, and be at rest."

When I was a teenager, my father uprooted the family and moved us to the state of Washington where he had found employment. At first it was exciting — traveling through many states, seeing historic sights and scenic places we had read about. Daddy had made a couple of trips "Out West," as he called it, and he had spun many wondrous tales to us about it. The state of Washington was a great disappointment to us, at least in the part where we located.

The restless wind blew across the desert, gigantic balls of tumbleweed rolled about, and there were no trees to rest one's eyes. The younger children enrolled in school, where they were viewed as strange specimen. People laughed at our "hillbilly" language, and we were truly fish out of water. I remember my brothers crying out to Daddy, " Please take us home — we'll grub sprouts or anything!" The people there were as strange to us as we were to them. Rootless, wandering families who traveled from job to job, they had spawned a generation of adolescents who were a mixture of sophistication and ignorance. They were worldly, yet knew nothing about the elemental values of life. Oh, we were so out of place.

Daddy took pity on us and brought us home. I strongly suspect that he, too, was homesick for hills. After a few months of living in a strange land, we were back on the same farm. I am still here today.

Just what is it that binds us to these hills? One of the basic reasons is our deep sense of kinship. Here, you are known by your father and your grandfather. These roots are very important to us, this continuity with the generations that have gone on before us and the generations coming after. We know who we are because we know who trod the way before us. These roots are an underlying support that hold us to these hills.

My grandmother and grandfather settled here

on this rough piece of land, bringing with them his
aged father and mother. I feel my beginnings go deep
in this rocky soil to intertwine with the roots of the
sassafras, the sumac, and the gnarly dogwood.
Sometimes I think of Grandma, in her sunbonnet and
apron, planting seeds in the same garden patch that I
tend, and feel such a nearness to her that I can almost
speak to her.

Our roots go back even further, to the
Scots-Irish ancestors who settled these hills and
valleys back in the 1700s. They found the freedom
and isolation they were longing for, and their heritage
has been passed down to us today. They had to be a
tough, self-reliant people to survive here, and we still
treasure this way of life. In the midst of modern
society, it is possible to live a relatively independent
way of life up one of these hollers.

It doesn't take too much to make a true
mountaineer happy — a warm home, a good coon dog,
a garden patch, and plenty of room around him. He
can raise a patch of corn for cornmeal, and he doesn't
need much else. I feel that I have the best of two
worlds. My children were privileged to attend a modern
high school, we are in close driving distance of a city,
and yet I am only minutes away from the deep solitude
of the woods and hills. I am content.

The inexpressible beauty of the mountains is
another link in the chain that binds us here. Spring
will soon be waking up the hills. Down in the soft
mud, wild flowers are beginning to stir and send forth
tiny tendrils. Underneath the dry fronds of the
creeping phlox, bright green shoots are forming. The
cheery "cheeter-cheeter" of the cardinal is heard in the

early morning, and will soon be joined by other songbirds. Springtime in the hills cannot be adequately described — it must be absorbed.

Soon the hills will come alive with the radiant hue of the redbud trees, contrasting with the pure white blossoms of the dogwood. The trees will raise their green banners to the sky,and the mountains will teem with new life. There is so much varied beauty in this state. Nowhere is there such a variety of wild flowers as here in the hills. It takes a common people who live close to the earth to appreciate the delicate white violet as it blooms shyly from a crevice in a rock. The wild anemones are among the first wild flowers to bloom, as they spring up among last year's dead leaves and tremble in the slightest breeze. Everywhere there will be bluets, violets, and the scattered coin of the dandelion.

There are majestic mountain peaks, towering rock formations, and clear mountain streams. The hills flaunt their greenness in summer, and unmatched glory in autumn; they raise bare, angular arms to the sky in winter, and early spring covers the same bare arms with an aura of soft, developing leaves. In all seasons, they fairly shout with beauty.

I was born and nurtured in these hills, and I hope to end my days here. I climb the hill to the cemetery beside the church, both built on Grandpa's land, and pause beside my grandparents' graves. From this vantage point, I can see where my children have built and settled on this same land. I hear the joyous shouts of my grandchildren as they romp and play in the woods below me, and see the same creek that I splashed in as a child. To my left is my mother's house where, fiercely independent, she lives alone.

Blood that flowed through my grandparents' veins is now coursing through my children and grandchildren, generation after generation. The giant beech that towers over my grandparents' graves has surely wrapped its roots around their bones, anchoring them even more securely to the land. The past seems to echo down through the years as the voices of my grandchildren grow fainter, and I think, "These are my people — this is where I belong."

INTRODUCTION

More than fifty years ago, I was born in an old, rough, two-story house that nestled on the banks of Big Laurel Creek, Clay County, West Virginia. This was my mother's home place, where her parents, Abner Jehu and Laura Alice Samples had lived and raised eleven children. My life there beside that deep, rushing stream that emptied into Elk River was of short duration; when I was a year old, my parents moved back to my grandfather's farm on Summer's Fork. Summer's Fork, also called Ovapa, was the small creek that ran into Little Laurel Creek, which in turn flowed into Big Laurel Creek.

My grandfather O'Dell had brought his family, including his parents, to this rocky little farm from Nicholas County. The gas and oil drillers had swarmed into this vicinity at that time, making Ovapa a boom town. But by the time I was born, the nation was still in the aftermath of the Great Depression, and work was as scarce as money. Times were hard as I was growing up; yet I don't recall any deprivation or real hardship. I do remember the love and security of a large, close-knit family, neighbors who were kind and helpful, neighbor's children who grew up with us and formed lifetime bonds. I attended a two-room school for eight years, where strong moral principles were taught along with the ABC's. We were taken to church and Sunday School almost as soon as we were born, and the foundation for spiritual strength was laid there. We grew up in a clean country atmosphere; ran free in the woods and fields. All of these things combined to make us the men and women we are today.

My children were raised in much the same setting. We built on the family farm, produced a total of six children (four of them established homes on this same piece of property) and eleven of our fourteen grandchildren live in sight of us. A couple of years ago, with the children all gone from the nest, we built a home on almost the exact spot where my old home sat.

Much is still the same, and yet there are some changes. The stock tanks that were lined up beside the road are gone, and the oil rigs that reached tall, metal pyramids to the sky have been replaced by pumping jacks. No more the loud "chug-chug" of their engine houses echo through the hills; silent too is the compressor station that puffed day and night all through my childhood. Sometimes, late in a summer evening, when the lavender shadows between the hollers turn to deeper purple, it seems you can hear the worried voice of a mother calling "Coda — Coda!", but there is no answer . . .

None of us ever dreamed our lives would turn out as they have. We never figured on growing older when we were children playing on the Virginia office porch, skinning the cat on the iron pipes, and forming our secret clubs in the barn. It seemed that life would go on forever, just the same, when we were kids growing up on Summer's Fork . . .

SOFTLY COMES SPRING

Just like a little lamb, March came in on soft feet this morning. The puffy white clouds that floated, lamblike, across the sky yesterday are gone. The vast expanse of sky stretches, blue and cloudless, over our hills and ridges. The earth is waiting, with breathless expectancy, for the warming kiss of the sun to bring sleeping nature back to life. Our own bodies feel the pull to get out, to rake, or clean or do something. We used to rake the garden this time of year, and pile the cornstalks and refuse from last year's crops into a heap and burn off the garden. The idea was to burn the insects and pests along with clearing the garden patch, but now the flattop mower makes short work of chopping up the cornstalks and weeds and the mulch is simply plowed under. But I miss the burning smell of spring.

We are getting ready to hatch out some baby chickens, but we are using an incubator instead of waiting for a broody hen to "go to settin'." Just as the flattop mower has replaced the old garden rake, the incubator has replaced the mother hen. But the chickens turn out to be the same little bright-eyed balls of fluff, and we substitute a lot of mother love. Last year we hatched out several chickens, and also a bunch of small bantam chickens. When my husband's sister visited in the summer, she brought along some of her grandchildren who had been raised strictly in the city. Five-year-old Benji was enthralled with the baby chickens. He examined the baby Leghorns for quite some time, then I showed him the baby banties in their cages, and told him they were banties. He silently studied them for a few minutes, then with the air of one who is the bearer of bad news but is reluctant to tell it, remarked gravely, "Aunt Alyce, I'm afraid these are going to grow up and be chickens!"

How blessed our children are to live close to the land and the beauties of nature! I think being close to nature makes us closer to God. How can we view the swelling buds on the lilac bush, hear the cardinal burst into his song of praise, feel the warming rays of the sun on our faces, and not be aware of a great and loving Father who made all of this?

This is the time of year when Mom used to dig out the feedsacks to make us some spring clothes. Before the days of plastic sacks and paper bags, animal feed was purchased in cotton sacks of every pattern and color. Most country kids knew what it was to be decked out in a feedsack dress or shirt. Mom used the white ones to make our gowns and petticoats, and also our bloomers. We were proud of our print dresses and skirts, but at Easter time Mom always made sheer dotted swiss dresses with tiers, ruffles and lace. With our black patent Mary Janes and new white socks, we felt as if we had "done died and gone to heaven." The boys got new cowboy shirts and western jeans, and a new cowboy hat. This would fit in right now, but then they stuck out like a sore thumb. Daddy loved the western outfits, however, and the boys wore them proudly.

I'll never forget the Easter when a neighboring family saved enough feedsacks to make all their boys a shirt alike. Unfortunately, the print happened to be bright red flowers on a green background. The little boys looked like a row of Mallard ducks trailing after their mother.

Kids today have so much that they have lost the thrill of knowing, after a steady diet of feedsack clothes, how it feels to get that one new outfit. It seems that we are all like that; the more we have the less thankful we are. God has blessed America with plenty, but she is spiritually destitute. We need to remember that "a man's life consisteth not in the abundance of the things which he possesseth."

The Clay Free Press
March 3, 1982

The evening sky glows a pearly pink, forming a backdrop for trees made of pure white lace. It is a pink and white world, and the most spectacular snowfall I have ever seen. Heavy snow clings to every twig in the forest, and the bare trees are bowed down under a burden nearly as heavy as the pines. The branches interlacing overhead form a canopy that shuts out the sky and produces the sensation of walking through a white tunnel. It is a world of indescribable beauty, of gossamer white stretching as far as the eye can see — truly a fairyland. You may be sick and tired of snow, but no one can deny the breath-taking beauty of it all.

The snowdrops and crocuses are blooming under this thick blanket of white, waiting patiently for their day in the sun. And it will come. We, too, must be patient.

A dear old friend of mine chided me mildly for telling about the feedsack underwear we used to wear. She confessed that when she was a girl they also wore the feedsack petticoats and bloomers (only they called them "drawers") but they were ashamed and didn't tell anyone. At the time I wore them, I probably didn't broadcast the fact, but now I think it is funny. Still, I don't remember ever feeling particularly poor or underprivileged, as most people around us lived pretty much on the same scale.

If my dear old friend felt bad about her feedsack drawers, she should consider my Aunt Addie. She had a pair, that if she bent over too far, exposed the lettering "White Feed" right across the bottom. At least ours were all white.

The year that I graduated from high school, we were going through a lean spell. It seemed that every evening when the school bus pulled up beside our house, Mom would be out picking wild greens. I was mortified at first, then it got to be a joke that Mom was out getting our supper. I still love greens.

I remember starting to high school in a beautiful tiered dress made of thin, red print material, topped off with a black pin striped suit jacket. I wore it proudly, and if there were snickers behind my back, I was blissfully unaware of it.

We were rich in the things that really counted. We had a mother and father that loved one another dearly, and we knew we were loved and wanted. This is a security that no money or worldly possessions can buy. We had plenty to eat, even if it was rough country grub — and that is still the best kind. Our clothes were warm, if not fashionable, and Daddy spent much time with us kids. The hunting and fishing trips will always be a warm memory. Most of all, we were brought up in the way of the Lord. We were taught to love and reverence God, and above all to be faithful to Him. I am sure that our flock of young'ens have not forgotten Daddy, and his prayers.

The Clay Free Press
March 10, 1982

My Aunt Ruby kept open house all day long on Sunday when her family was all home. I loved to go there. It was a ritual that wherever we went on Sunday, we would stop at Aunt Ruby's on the way home. Criss and I were much younger then, with only a couple of little ones to drag along, and there were very few Sundays that we missed going there. When you stopped, you couldn't get away without eating. It seems odd now, but I can't remember what the furniture looked like, or the color of the walls, but I can still feel that warm welcome that reached out and enveloped us. I remember the food too — big cookers of fresh half runner beans in the summertime, pots of chicken and fat, yellow dumplings, and spaghetti and meatballs. Aunt Ruby made a molasses-black walnut cake that would cure anything from heartache to the "blahs." It was several layers high, put together with spicy, sweetened applesauce. She left the food out on the table, so that whoever stopped by could eat to their heart's content. There were several cousins who made their rounds, and we were all treated the same.

Aunt Ruby and Uncle Tommy loved young people. The youngsters around here formed a 4-H club, and their meetings were held in Uncle Tommy's cellar top. Aunt Ruby, the adult leader, popped the popcorn and made the cookies. I remember so many things — "Old Restful," the rock where we kids rested as we climbed the steep hill after the cows, the attic with its many treasures, and the fat pet groundhog that was almost a member of the family. One thing I can't remember though is a harsh or grouchy word out of either one of them.

The house is gone now; burned a long time ago. Uncle Tommy is gone too, and the children are all married and have children — and grandchildren — of their own. A house trailer stands now where the old house once stood. Sometimes, though, when I pass by, I can almost see the two story, white house, with the dog Tubby lying on the porch. And if I glance quick enough, there is Oscar the groundhog crying because the chickens have taken his bread again. Some things you never forget.

Criss's chicken hobby has really blossomed. The thin, piping crow of the Old English white banty rooster wakens us at four o'clock, echoed by the hoarser cry of the red Cochin, and multiplied by eight or ten others. Our conversation centers around black and white Japanese silkies, Golden Seabrights and black Rosecombs. I'm probably the only woman in the county who has two incubators perched on her chest of drawers, and is lulled to sleep by the syncopated beat of their thermostats kicking on and off.

I looked the other day, and I do believe that I am growing feathers on my feet.

The Clay Free Press
March 17, 1982

The little spring peepers that have been sending their spring salute heavenward have burrowed back into the soft mud of the pond for a brief nap. These last few days, March has been showing some lionlike teeth. Its ferocious temperament is pretty much of a bluff, though, as I saw the sun shining brightly while the snow was coming down furiously. From all indications, March will be taking its leave like a gentle lamb.

It is lawn raking time again, and nothing seems so satisfying as fine-combing the lawn with a leaf rake. The new grass seems to stretch and breathe as the old dead grass and debris are raked away. To have a lovely yard has always been one of my ambitions. It used to be dotted with tricycles, bicycles, wagons, dogs, assorted children, and even a pony staked out occasionally. Now that the children are mostly grown up and gone, it is simply decorated with tricycles, bicycles, wagons, dogs, banty pens and assorted grandchildren. I do have a beautiful weeping willow tree started in the far corner of the yard. So far it has been used as the goal post in several football games, stopped a runaway go-cart with a three-year-old at the wheel and supported the target for bow and arrow practice. It is listing a little toward the south, but its graceful branches are putting forth tiny green leaves. It is hopeful, and so am I. I can always look forward to the retirement years, and tottering about on feeble feet plucking a stray dead leaf from my cherished lawn — and dodging the tricycles, bicycles, wagons, dogs, etc. — and assorted great-grandchildren.

We have been cleaning the outbuildings; sorting and hauling away accumulated litter. There are two things that Criss and I can't do in harmony. One is plant a garden together. The hoeing and cultivating we can do peacefully — but that initial planting is where the rub comes in. He wants to take a bucketful of onion sets and pour them out in a row, while I like to place each set, root down, exactly three inches apart. I generally stalk off in extreme exasperation, to reappear later with "I told you so," when fifty-five onions appear in a six inch space.

The other thing is on what to discard when we are cleaning. We are both savers, but in different ways. I can't bear to throw away any kind of papers. Just about a year ago, I finally burned our utility receipts for 1955. Who knows when you might need these things? I have my oldest son's first grade papers, and he will be 39 in May. Criss fusses some about it, so the other day I got up enough nerve to throw away a tool catalog that had been outdated for three years. The next day he asked for it.

The things he saves seem ridiculous to me. I picked up a junky-looking metal object and started to toss it on the discards. "Don't throw that away — it's the dinglewhiffle for a thermopop." (At least that's what it sounded like he said.) "I might need it for the car," he yelled. Reluctantly I put it back with three more dinglewhiffles, some dryer parts, and other mysterious objects that he might need someday. I passed the shop door where he had piled a small truck load of things he was throwing away and spied the legs to the table we had bought for Crystal when she was small. "I want these," I said firmly as I dug them out of the pile. "I am going to put that back together." He fixed a steely eye on me and said grimly, "If you touch one thing in that pile I am going to quit!" I slunk back in the house and shut my eyes as he hauled the stuff away.

I guess it's true that one man's meat is an other woman's poison.

The Clay Free Press
March 31, 1982

Winter seems reluctant to give up its grip on our Clay County hills and ridges, but hangs around like a guest who has stayed too long — Grandpa O'Dell used to say "plumb wore out his welcome." I saw creeping phlox peeping out from a frosting of snow, their little mauve and rose colored heads braving the freezing temperatures. Rows of bright tulips and daffodils stand at attention, their backbones stiffened by icy winds and blowing snow. Grandson David demanded this week, "When is spring, Mommaw — when?" I think a lot of adults are beginning to echo the same thought.

Some of the hardier ones in our family took their campers and mushed to William's River for a few days of camping and fishing. We are supposed to join them there next week, but this cold weather has just about bluffed me out. The older my bones get, the louder they holler for a soft bed and a nice warm house. I do love to camp out though, especially in the fall. There is always hope that it will warm up — I have never seen anything like this weather. There were several windy tales that surfaced; some of which I took with a grain of salt. It really did blow a cinder block off my mom's house — it was on the roof holding down a loose shingle. Someone told me it played havoc with their chickens — that it blew a rooster into a gallon jug, and one old hen laid the same egg three times. It did blow one of our banty pens, containing four pairs of bantams, into the creek. When we rescued them, they were cackling hysterically and "madder than a wet hen."

There are many things to be thankful for — the power stayed on, this is the ending of winter instead of the beginning, and I have already had the chicken pox. This scratchy disease is making its rounds among my grandchildren and the neighborhood children as well. I told four year old Benji that Jeremy had given the chicken pox to Aaron, and he was indignant. "I ain't taking them — not from nobody," he told me in no uncertain terms.

The Clay Free Press
April 14, 1982

The dogtooth violets are blooming along the banks of William's River. They gleam like yellow stars from their beds of dry pine needles, surrounded by the delicate lace of the maidenhair fern. The air is still crisp and pure here, and the water runs swift and icy. There is nothing more soothing than to spend a few days away from the hurry and bustle of everyday living, getting close to nature.

I sat on one of the immense boulders that seem

flung with abandon along the banks and in the bed of the river, and marveled at the wonderful works that the mighty hand of God has wrought. The sun brought out the warm, piney scent of the hemlocks that grow right down to the water's edge, and the rhododendron leaves dipped and fluttered in the breeze. The river rushed on at my feet, swirling around rocks and fallen trees, to meet and crest in foamy white curls. I felt at peace with God and man.

How Daddy loved to camp and fish here! As far back as I can remember, we made frequent voyages to Williams, Cherry and Cranberry Rivers, and the Back Fork of Elk. In my musings, I could almost see him rounding the bend in the river, his old fishing hat stuck full of dry flies, and the wicker creel on his side full of moist ferns and the trout that he had caught. The familiar smile was on his face as he proudly displayed the big brown trout that almost got away.

Daddy is gone now, but the river flows on just the same. If the world stands, there will come a time when I will no longer sit on the banks of William's River and watch the swirl and eddy of the water. I hope my children will remember and say, "How she loved this place!" But even more important, I hope they will remember how I loved God who made all this. And still the river will flow on, until God calls time to a halt.

The grandchildren took to camping like baby ducks to a pond. The first day we were up there, six inches of snow fell on Kennison Mountain. It rained, and sleeted, and they thrived. Every grandson I had fell, at least once, into the little stream that ran beside their camp. It was fed by melting snow and was pure ice water. It didn't hurt any of them.

The day we came back home, we decided to leave early in order to get back for prayer meeting that night. Mom wanted to fish some more, as she hadn't caught anything that week. While I was cooking our noon meal, she decided she would cut across a wide bottom beside the camp and fish a little longer. There was a beautiful collie dog that had adopted us while we were there, and she called him to go with her. She was gone just a short while when Criss happened to glance out the window to see Mom running hard away from the river and across the bottom, with the collie at her heels. He stopped every few minutes to turn and bark furiously at the river bank. Criss ran outside and heard Mom gasp, "Bear!" He ran as hard as he could, with the kids tearing along behind him hoping to get a look at the dangerous animal. When he got to the river bank, he could see a black, bulky object on the other side, partly hidden by thick rhododendron bushes. While he watched, the vicious animal turned and gave a definite "Moo!" It was a big Black Angus cow.

Mom explained weakly to Criss that she wasn't afraid, but she thought it might swim the river and jump on the dog. Criss asked her if she was so concerned about the dog, how come she ran off and left him?

Mom won't even let us sing, "The bear went over the mountain."

The Clay Free Press
April 21, 1982

March has mellowed, with the coming of spring right upon us. Today the sun streams down from a brilliant blue sky, coaxing the buds on the lilac bush to loosen their tight grip. The spring peepers have again started their exuberant springtime orchestra, making music from every pond and low marshy place.

It may not sound like music to a stranger to our hills, but to us natives who have survived another West Virginia winter, it is sweet music indeed. The air is still nippy, but the sun's rays have a decided warmth as they touch the earth. The land is beginning to waken from the long sleep of winter. The last week of March slides away and spring hovers close — so close.

It is with relief that I read in the paper that a psychiatry professor from WVU asserts that spring fever is a real malady, not a fantasy. I am so glad — all these years I thought the dreamy, sleepy state of mind in the spring was simply laziness. He says that spring fever is a hangover from winter. Now I have an excuse to sit for hours on the soft new grass and stare at a daffodil.

At one time, the cure for spring fever was a whopping dose of sulphur and molasses. We never had to endure that, but if we sneezed or looked cross-eyed, we were subjected to a dose of the nastiest stuff known to kids — castor oil. I plainly remember that throat-gagging, stomach-turning medication today. No matter what ailed us, I am sure that the cure was worse than the disease. I take my spring tonic in the form of a cup of hot sassafras tea now.

Another demeaning springtime treatment was our annual "deworming." Never mind whether we had worms or not, we all had to take part in the ritual. A childhood friend of mine recalls the three big pink pills that the children in her family had to take. She hated them so much that she hid hers in the crevice of a big sycamore tree. She stated that she might still have worms, but the tree is graveyard dead.

Spring affects people in various ways. Son Andy has been practicing his turkey calls until he can hardly speak English. His brother Kevin tried out one of his calls, and his eyes bulged out, his face turned beet red, and the cords in his neck swelled. Criss told him that he doubted if a turkey would respond, but he could probably steal chickens.

Spring has tiptoed so softly into our hills that at first we were almost unaware of her presence. There has been an almost imperceptible softening of the tree limbs, and the first fuzzy buds appear. In the woods, new life is forming as the first tender plants appear. Through the dead, dry leaves of last year, the pale, delicate blooms of the wood anemone tremble in the light breeze. The deeply lobed leaves of the wild geranium are visible now although the lavender flowers have not yet appeared. Through the rich humus, the tightly curled umbrellas of the Mayapple poke through, ready to be unfurled when April sends her showers. The miracle of life begins anew as the sun kisses the cold, barren earth and causes it to blossom.

Dawn breaks on a cloudless sky, as the cheerful "cheeter-cheeter" of a cardinal pierces the air. Mornings are clear and cold, but the warm rays of the sun soon bring the yellow and black swallowtail butterfly on the wing, and coaxes out the shy blue face of the violet. It is sheer pleasure to see spring unfold in our hills and valleys. The scripture in 2 Samuel says it best, "And he shall be as the light of the morning, when the sun riseth, even as a morning without clouds; as the tender grass springing out of the earth by clear shining after rain."

Have you ever noticed what a close affinity exists between little boys and creeks? Despite repeated warnings, three-year-old Luke managed to fall from our bridge to the creek beneath, landing on his head. He was unhurt, other than being cold, wet and completely outraged. He was promptly rescued by his Uncle Kevin, who popped him in a tub of warm water. In spite of the first-hand lesson, a couple of day later five-year-old David ventured too close to the creek and was taken home dripping wet. Peggy soundly raked him over the coals, ending her lecture with, "And I don't even have a dryer to dry your clothes." David listened in solemn silence, then said gravely, "I'll tell you one thing, Mommy, when I grow up and have kids they better think twice before they do things like this!"

The warm sunshine this week has dried up the gardens until they are ready for planting. All up and down our holler, I see the age-old ritual of potato planting — the scattering of the fertilizer, the bending and dropping of the cut potato, and the patient covering with dirt; done with perfect faith that God will send the rain and sunshine to make the crops grow.

The Clay Free Press
April 18, 1985

Betty Marie was always a fighter. As far back as I can remember, in the dim and distant land of my grade school days, Betty was there. Nobody pushed her around, and nobody pushed her friends around. She always took up for the underdog, and she wasn't afraid of anyone. The school bully sported a bloody nose more than once, and the biggest boy in school learned to step softly around her. And she was so much fun! Anytime there was a practical joke, you can be sure that she was right in the middle of it. She had a hearty laugh that rang out unrestrained, and there was a joy of living that rubbed off on others. Betty Marie was the girl who upset Mr. Hinkle, the grade school principal. She rode her sleigh into his legs and rode him backward all the way down the hill.

With all the fun there was about her, she was also a worker. She would tackle housework (which most of us girls tried to avoid) with a zest and then look for more to do. Mom loved having her in our home. She not only would wash all the dishes, but would mop the floor too. We went on to grade school, then on to high school together, and Betty stayed the same happy, carefree person. After graduation, she married and moved to New York, and we went our separate ways. I didn't see her for several years, and one day she stopped by to see me. I could hardly believe it was the same person. The tomboy had turned into a slender, attractive woman — and she was so pretty. After we started reminiscing about the good old times past, I discovered that she had the same big, hearty laugh and the same merry heart.

We saw each other on and off through the years, and there was a special joy about her. She had found a real experience with the Lord, and all she could talk about was how she loved to go to church. Some time after that visit, her mother told me that Betty had found lumps in her neck. This was the beginning of the biggest battle she had ever fought.

The lumps were malignant, and she underwent surgery in 1974. She made a good recovery and was able to be home for some time. However, the battle raged on unseen in her body. As time went on, she grew worse, and then it was radiation and chemotherapy. She fought courageously and hard. Then there was treatment so new that it was virtually unheard of in this country. She kept her deep faith in God, and her cheery outlook. The day before she went to the hospital for the last time, she told a close friend, "Wherever I go, He goes with me." (Yea, though I walk through the valley of the shadow of death, I will fear no evil for Thou art with me.) She fought valiantly right up to the end. Even then, death was not the victor. God, in His infinite love and mercy, decided that she had fought long and hard enough, and tenderly reached down and took her out of the battle. (O, death, where is thy sting? O, grave, where is thy victory?) There is no sting when God takes one of his own.

The Clay Free Press
March 24, 1982

April came back to reclaim her moon, and hopefully took the last of the winter weather with her. The rain that fell last night already has a softer, more gentle quality — the kind that calls forth the flowers of May. The songbirds blend their voices in sweet harmony at daybreak, and the air is full of the sounds of spring. A mother robin hovers over her nest of little ones in the grape arbor and lets me approach quite near, although she watches me warily with a bright, beady eye. Our resident chipmunk is seen every day, scurrying between the corn crib and the creek bank, going about his everyday chipmunk business. The redbud is beginning to bloom, contrasting with the white blossoms of the dogwood. God has softened our Clay County hills with the greening touch of spring.

Spring house cleaning time has overtaken us, and a few energetic housewives have completed theirs. I like to wait until the fire in the woodstove can be discontinued, and then, of course, I want to stay outside. I would rather cut and pile brush than clean house, but it is a necessary evil and must be faced. I remember how Daddy used to admonish us when we were kids at home, "If you dread to do a job, get right into it and finish it, then you can do something else." He would get perturbed when we would procrastinate in doing the dishes, and we could make a four hour job out of it. Our water had to be carried from a hand pump outdoors, and stored in zinc buckets placed on a special table called "the water table." We had a long handled dipper in one of the buckets to drink from. Dish water was heated in two large aluminum dishpans on the kitchen stove, and two girls were delegated to do the washing and drying. With four daughters, Mom did the cooking and we did the cleaning up afterward. My downfall was the old outdoor johnny house, where I always had a book hidden. (It was overhead, Mom, underneath a piece of the tin roofing.) Of course I had to go there while the dish water was heating and devour several chapters of the current book. When I got back, the water was too hot. Then I had to go back again while the water cooled off. Sometimes this cycle would be repeated until I finished a whole book. But Mom would outwait us and we had to do our task no matter how long it took. Crystal uses the same tactic on me, but I usually get irritated and do the thing myself — and I shouldn't. She really is allergic to detergents, so I bought her a pair of rubber gloves. She must be allergic to them too, as she has used them once.

Early one morning Mom sent Mark and Ronnie, my youngest brothers, to the garden to hoe. They were grown boys — young men really — with an old car minus a motor that they pushed around. They shoved the car to the upper end of the garden and supposedly began their gardening chores. Along about ten o'clock Mom looked out, and seeing absolutely no movement, decided to investigate. She slipped up on the old car, and sure enough, both boys and Freckles the dog were fast asleep. Mom cut a switch, and opening the car door just wide enough to accommodate her arm, poured it on both the boys. She gave the dog some of her birch tea, too. They finished the garden.

Children need to be taught to finish a task, no matter how unpleasant it may be. I must be still

learning; so I'd better hunt the scrub brush and begin.
The Clay Free Press
April 28, 1982

Friendship is a gift of God, and the friendships
that have lasted down through the years are a special
blessing. Remembrance is a golden chain that the
years and miles cannot break.

Peggy Ann (Hanshaw) Courtney came
unexpectedly to visit last week, and it was one of the
best surprises that I have had in a long time. It was
the first time I had seen her in ten years or so. All
through our growing up years, Peggy Ann was as dear
and familiar as a sister to me. We went through grade
school together, and then all four years of high school.
Much time was spent in each other's homes, and our
lives were entwined together. We spent a couple of
hours reminiscing about the good old times past,
shared much laughter and a few tears. Then she and
her husband got into their big Cadillac to travel back
to their stately home in Tampa. I climbed into our old
'69 Ford pickup and journeyed to Clay to do a few
chores. I felt the roots of my life grow a little deeper
into this country soil, and take hold a little more
tenaciously. She is happy in her world, and I am
content in mine. But when the circle of our worlds
meet, there is a pull on the heart strings.

We have nine grandchildren five years of age
and under — six of them boys, and they all live within
sight of our house. The things that happen are
unbelievable.

On a typical evening last week, daughter Patty
and I were watching Jeremy and my niece Julie
through the picture window. They were on the bridge

going through a cheerleading routine. Just as Jeremy stepped up on the bridge railing, I gasped, "Oh, that's where his daddy fell and cut his head open when he was little!" Patty said, "He just fell off, Mom."

When we pulled him out of the creek, soaked and bleeding, it looked as if his head was cut open from his forehead to his chin, and he was shaking uncontrollably from shock and the cold water. When we finally got the blood and tears stanched enough to inspect the damage, we found that he had hit his nose and lip on a piece of angle iron sticking out from the bridge. We told him it was a good thing that he didn't have a nose like his Poppaw Criss or he'd still be hanging there. Aaron had been fishing in the creek, and during this commotion managed to snag a fishhook in my earlobe. When Patty tried to take it loose, she found that it had been baited with a big wad of well-chewed, pink bubblegum. Just then we saw David trotting down the road from his trailer, carrying his little plastic play doctor kit. In all seriousness, he strode up to Jeremy and said soberly, "Here, Brother, I brought my doctor kit!"

My sister, who is a nurse at the local health clinic, told me that a little boy confided to her that his sister takes "Appalachian fits." I bet that's what I've been having for years when the weather gets warm and I want to get outside in the woods and fields instead of doing my housework. I know a good treatment, though — poke greens. Criss and I picked a mess of them yesterday, and I cooked them with a piece of home-smoked bacon, made a pone of cornbread with home-ground meal, and ate it with a glass of buttermilk. It was flat dab good.

Get out and enjoy the spring — it's good for the soul.

The Clay Free Press
May 5, 1982

Mother's Day is almost upon us. I am glad that we have a day set aside to honor mothers, although they should be honored every day. It is so easy to take a mother for granted, just as if they will always be there. To our sorrow, we awaken to the realization that this is not so. I am blessed in having a mother who is physically energetic and has stayed young in mind. She has been a faithful example of love to her children, grandchildren and great grandchildren. My own children will bypass me to call on her for help and counsel — just as I still do. (Prov. 31:28 - "Her children rise up and call her blessed.")

Woman's Lib to the contrary, I feel that motherhood is the most noble calling that a woman can have. God has ordained a perfect plan for a happy home that places a woman in a position that no one else can fill. Oh, I know that it doesn't feel very noble at times. Those first few weeks when you bring a new baby home from the hospital can be a nightmare. After you finally get the newborn to sleep by feeding, rocking, shushing, and finally praying, you spend the rest of the night checking him to see if he is still breathing. But there is nothing to compare with the feel of a soft, tiny baby in your arms; the touch of his fuzzy head on your lips. There is an awesome awareness that this tiny scrap of humanity is **your** responsibility. Then comes the toddler days with bumps and scrapes becoming daily routine. And don't forget the teething pains, the mysterious fevers, and endless rashes that sometimes turn out to be chicken pox or scarlatina. There are mountains of diapers to be laundered and bottles to be washed and formula fixed. (Although I didn't fool too much with bottles, thanks to the example of a wise mother.) About the time he hits the terrible twos, there is another little one on the way. As I look back now, it seems that the early years of my motherhood were taken up with Pablum, laundry and the rocking chair. If this sounds grim, I can assure you that there were many blessings along the way. After a particularly hectic day, a pair of tiny arms around your neck and a whispered, "I love you better'n anybody!" made the difference.

Then comes the school years and that choked feeling when the first one starts to school. The years seem to flow one into another as they grow up before your eyes. Don't forget the trips to the dentist, the eye doctor, and the department store for the piles of clothing they are forever outgrowing. The adolescent period is a trial for parent and teenager alike, but they do grow up, and it is still a source of wonder to me that they become responsible, caring adults.

Yet, their physical needs, the financial drain, and their proper schooling are not our main responsibility. From the time God gives them to us as tiny babies, we must realize that this is a soul that we are responsible for. We alone must bear the burden of teaching them that they are responsible to God for their actions. How many have failed in this! If we neglect to do this in the formative years of their lives, when their minds are young and tender, we have failed them completely.

To successfully nurture an abiding faith in a child, it is imperative that we first find this faith for ourselves. Then it is our duty, nay, a privilege to teach the things of God to our children. The Bible gives the most solemn admonition to parents: "to bring up a child in the way that he should go, and when he is older he will not depart from it." In other words, the teaching will never leave him.

It is a beautiful thing to see parents training their children in God's way. In this world of changing values and shifting morals, our children need a firm foundation to build their character upon. I am glad that the word of God never changes. The ten commandments are as vital to us today as in the ancient days. The principles and morals taught by Christ will never be outdated. Our children must be taught these things.

I wish to pay homage to mothers everywhere, and especially to those godly mothers who are striving to give their children the most precious gift they can bestow — an unshakable faith in a loving Lord.

The Clay Free Press
May 9, 1984

One of Ovapa's own came home to stay this past week.

As far back as I can remember, there was the general store and post office — and there was Opal. She not only ran the store, but the post office as well. All the time I was growing up, she was there; when I married we built directly across the creek from her store. Our children grew up beside the store and Opal. When our daughter Patty was small, she thought Opal was one of her grandmothers. Opal was probably one of the best known, and certainly one of the most loved, women in our neighborhood.

Most communities had a general store, and hers was truly an old timey one where you could purchase everything from wash tubs to stock feed to groceries. Canned goods and packaged food were lined up in shelves all along one whole wall, while down the other side glass showcases held dry goods, thread, toiletries and patent medicines. As youngsters, we bought birthday presents there, orange blossom perfume, red brilliantine and Bay Rum shaving lotion. The soft drink cooler was located behind the counter, and above it was the tobacco section with cartons of cigarettes, plugs of Brown Mule chewing tobacco, and bags of Mail Pouch. The dairy and meat cases were lined up on the right and the candy case was beside it. A door to the feed room was on the right corner, where sacks of horse and mule feed, dog and dairy feed, and shovels, rakes and hoes were kept. Overhead hung the big wash tubs (which no household could do without), zinc water buckets, lanterns and dishpans. I barely remember the old gas tanks, with the glass bowl on top, but the kerosene tank was still in use. Everything to sustain a household was contained in that little store.

There was such a good mingled smell as you walked in the door. Opal would slice big round slices of Longhorn cheese from the huge wheel of cheese (and always popped a little piece in her mouth), wrap it in white paper, and tie it with twine. Where else could you buy a nickel's worth of lunch meat? Her patience was boundless; she would stand for long minutes while we clutched our pennies in hot, sweaty palms and agonized over whether to buy the root beer barrels or the jaw breakers. She always gave full measure, heaped up and running over. After her long, hard day was over and the store locked, there was rarely an evening when someone didn't "go around back" and ask her to go in for something they needed. The school children gathered there every morning to stay warm while they waited for the bus to run. Opal gave out credit until it hurt, then went the second mile. I can see her now, jotting down purchases on her bill pad, chewing the tip of her tongue as she concentrated. I am sure there are uncollected accounts to this day, forgiven and forgotten.

Through it all, I never saw her lose patience with anyone or become the least bit cranky. If she complained, we never heard her. She not only gave out the mail, she gave out loans, friendship and lots of love. No matter what the circumstances, she kept a cheery smile on her face. She always had the ability to laugh at her problems and sympathize with yours. When she retired and moved to Clay, we not only lost a general store — we lost a true friend as well.

I miss the old country store with its diversity of goods. I miss the post office in the corner, with its old wooden bench to sit on while the mail was being sorted. It was a gathering place for most of the community to meet and exchange gossip, talk about the crops and weather, and listen for their names to be called as Opal distributed the mail. The country store and homey post office are almost a thing of the past, a relic of a bygone era. But most of all I miss Opal, and the kindness she dispensed along with the candy.

Gladys Opal Jarvis was laid to rest Sunday, February 9, 1992 in the Belcher Cemetery at Ovapa. She was 83 years old, and left a multitude of good memories behind.

The Charleston Gazette
February 21, 1992

The month of May is such a tender one. At no other time in the year do the leaves hang so soft and delicate. The year is in its youth, and all too soon it will pass into the middle age of summer and then the summer will be ended. Our own lives seem to rush by just as fast. I look at all these grandkids sometimes and wonder where the years have gone. I remarked to Mom how old I was feeling with my gray hair blowing in the breeze. She replied, "Humph, I'll tell you what makes you really feel old — it's to have a kid with hair as gray as yours!" Mom can always cheer a person.

The jack-in-the-pulpit is blooming now in woodsy places. He stands, erect and dignified, preaching his silent message to the woodland creatures. He is also called an Indian turnip, but don't try to eat one. One taste will do you for a lifetime. A thousand needles will pierce your tongue and your whole mouth will feel paralyzed. There were so many things in the woods that we tasted when we were children. We chewed birch twigs and spicewood bark. I can remember the oily taste of the spicewood berry and the berry on Solomon's seal is sweet and sticky. The pokeberry tastes sick and sumac berries are sour as whiz. Mountain tea is very tasty and so are its berries. We scouted the hills for deer berries, Mayapples and pawpaws. I have read that some of these things are considered toxic, but I am in good health — whether because of, or in spite of all these wood's delicacies.

Some of these things were not so pleasant to the taste buds, such as yellow root for the sore throat. Slippery elm bark that was used for the same purpose was not so bad, and Grandma Peach used to make a concoction from black oak bark, yellowroot, honey and various other herbs that would really cure a cough. Mom used poultices made from plantain leaves for our stone bruises and catnip tea for other ailments. We were a healthy bunch.

The Clay Free Press
May 19, 1982

If children are a blessing, then grandchildren are doubly so. We have been richly blessed.

I'll never forget our first grandchild, Jennifer Alyce. My namesake . . .

Our daughter Patty has always jumped into life with both feet. The word "wait" was never part of her vocabulary. She moves quickly, finishes her work promptly, and then searches eagerly for more to do. She has always been impulsive, quick-spoken, and a whirlwind of energy. When anyone in the family needs something done quickly, it is Patty we turn to. Sometimes I think she mothers me.

When she married at nineteen, she got pregnant almost immediately. Her older brother had been married for three years and hadn't started a family, but she didn't waste a minute. I was on pins and needles lest the baby be born a bit premature, and set tongues to wagging. I could hear Grandpa saying, "They turned the horse loose before they built the barn." I remember how hurt she was when she confided to me that she was expecting, and I blurted out that I wished she had waited for awhile. "Mommy," she said tearfully, "I thought you'd be as happy as I am!" I swallowed thoughts of finances, immaturity and other doubts and hugged her.

There was never a baby more wanted or planned for; Patty began sewing baby clothes, planning a nursery and eagerly waiting for her newborn. Her enthusiasm bubbled over to my young nieces and nephews, and they were all anxious for "Patty's baby." She blossomed during her pregnancy with that inner glow some women seem to obtain during that time. She took excellent care of her health and diet, refusing even an aspirin for a headache.

The baby chose her birth date exactly nine months and ten days after the wedding day. Full of enthusiasm, Patty would have taken the entire tribe for the event but settled for her parents, grandmother, husband, and the pastor and his wife. Her labor went on for more than twenty four hours; her father and the pastor and wife had to return home. We were all worn out when, in the wee hours of the morning, a seven pound seven ounce baby girl made her debut into the world.

Patty was exhausted but exultant, and Randy was as proud as if he had accomplished the deed all by himself. We got our first look at her in the nursery after she had been washed and dressed. She was plump and beautiful with her eyes closed in sleep, and a curl of dark hair crowning her little round head. I couldn't see her eyes.

Mom and I both noticed that she was rather blue, but when we questioned the obstetrician he assured us that she was just fine; he had checked her heart and it was probably just a temporary oxygen loss as she was being born — but he did order x-rays then. He told us to go on home and get some sleep, that it had been a long siege but Patty and the baby were doing fine.

As I drove back up the river, Mom and I were both concerned that the baby seemed too blue, but neither one of us entertained the thought that it might be something serious. I had been home only a few minutes when the telephone rang. I thought it was one of my brothers teasing me about becoming a new grandmother, but finally the words began to register in my tired mind. He was saying in a deep accent, "This is the surgeon, and the baby is in deep distress. We have to operate immediately." In a daze I called our pastor, and Criss and I hurried back to the hospital.

Randy had stayed with Patty, and the doctor had explained the baby's condition to them. It seemed that it was a rare birth defect, called a Bochdalek congenital hernia, which translated into layman terms meant that one lung had not developed. For some reason during the development of the fetus, when the diaphragm should have closed, it had not. The small intestine had drifted into the chest cavity, preventing the lung from developing. The surgery was to close the hernia and to insert a prosthetic graft in the abdominal wall to make room for the small intestine. Patty and Randy were like two bewildered children, overwhelmed by tragedy and holding on to one another. We prayed, and waited ...

The surgeon returned to tell us that the operation was over and he had done all he could do. No one offered much hope; the obstetrician also was cautious about her recovery. "You have to remember that a newborn's heart is only about the size of a walnut, and the defect has also involved the right ventricle," he cautioned. But she was a fighter; the nurses in the intensive care nursery laughed at how she would grab the oxygen mask and jerk it off her face. Patty refused to dry her milk; she was determined to breast feed her baby. One pediatrician gently explained that it might be weeks before Jennifer could nurse, but Patty was adamant. She informed him firmly that she would pump her milk for as long as necessary. Patty is the type of person who is impossible to keep at arm's length; in spite of himself the obstetrician became emotionally caught up in the whole situation. He was a great comfort to the whole family.

Everyone was encouraged the next morning. The baby had made it through the night and was improving. I got to visit her for a few minutes in intensive care; she looked like a helpless little animal trussed up with wires and tubes emerging from every imaginable portion of her body. She was hanging on for dear life to the hose to her ventilator, and screaming loudly with her eyes tightly shut. My heart stopped as I looked at the tiny bit of humanity — my own flesh and blood. The nurses were more optimistic and hope was renewed.

Mom and I stayed late, then stopped at the grocery store on the way home. I had a queer, nagging feeling that something was wrong, but tried to shrug it off and went on home. Criss was waiting for me when I pulled in the driveway. Patty had called and said something was drastically wrong. For the first time, she wasn't allowed in ICU to see the baby, and no one would tell her anything. We rushed back to the hospital, and as we neared Patty's room, we could hear her crying. One of our favorite nurses stopped me, and putting both arms around me whispered, "I'm so sorry — the baby expired."

She had lived a total of forty-one hours. The doctor let Patty come home with us that night, and she insisted on going to the wake and funeral. At the wake, she held up her young cousins to see her baby. I can still see Brian turning away and crying as if his heart would break. One of the hardest times came for me when I helped Patty take a shower and her milk was running down the front of her gown. "All this milk, Mommy, and no baby," she said sadly.

Jennifer was laid to rest in the family cemetery beside the church, close to Grandma and Grandpa O'Dell's graves. The spreading arms of the giant beech shelter her, and in the fall the golden leaves shower her with whispery kisses. I held her after she died; I hugged and rocked her. She felt just like any other newborn baby, except her little body grew colder and colder. I never did get to see her eyes.

The grandchildren came in quick succession

after Jennifer; the following month brought Jeremy, a quicksilver baby who learned to swim when he was only a few weeks old. His platinum hair disappeared when he got wet, then dried in a duck's tail on the back of his head. He did much to ease the heartache of Jennifer, and then in another month Patty was expecting again. The doctor had recommended that she try a couple of months after she lost Jennifer, as her emotional welfare was more important than her physical being at the time. The following year she produced healthy Aaron, then it was Benjamin (Andy's and Phyl's) followed the next month by Kevin's and Sarah's Joshua. Unbelievably, in five years we accumulated nine grandchildren, six of them boys. I remember the time we tried to take a snapshot of all six boys lined up on the sofa — they were like a litter of puppies rolling and tumbling. By the time we took Benji's fist out of David's curls, Josh had Aaron around the neck. Just then Jeremy tried to lift Luke, and they both tumbled down. We never did get order restored. For several years.

There are random memories that come to mind. When Luke was three — a delightful age, not old enough to be consciously cute, but out of the terrible twos — he collected string. He was fascinated with ropes, belts or anything that would tie a knot. When I took him to the grocery store once and tried to lift him out of the shopping cart, he was stuck tight. He had tied the strings of his windbreaker to the cart handle, and it took me five minutes to work him loose while the carryout boy patiently waited. There was nothing sacred. If his Poppaw took off his work shoes and set them down, he would later find them tied to the dog, the bedpost, and one time dangling off the bridge by their shoe laces.

There was the time we remodeled the bathroom.

In the midst of our extensive project, we had a visit from our insurance agent. He got out of his car, detoured around the cement mixer, and gingerly skirted the large pile of sand and gravel. After talking a few minutes, he asked to see the woodburning stove on the back porch. As he passed the camper, I saw him eyeballing our toilet sitting in the yard in all its pink splendor. I took a deep breath and opened the door to the screened-in back porch. We had stacked the contents of the bathroom there, plus paneling, sheetrock, and odds and ends. I brought him through the kitchen (the damage had already been done) past the glass shower doors leaning against the wall, and into the living room where Patty sat in the early stages of labor (her third baby.) I guess he felt safer on the front porch, so he went out and sat in the swing. When he got up to leave, he almost fell flat on his face. Luke had been playing at his feet, and had taken a length of grass rope and tied his ankles to the porch post.

As he pulled out in his car, I think he said, "Don't call me — I'll call you." It is hard to hear when a car is going that fast.

The Clay Free Press
May 18, 1983

May has spread a mantle of soft green over our hills and ridges. The tender, young leaves quiver in each vagrant breeze, and the sun adds its blessings after our recent rains. Along Elk River, growth is more abundant and the leaves are fuller. On the surface of the river, flocks of ducks float gracefully as they bob and dive for their dinner. Occasionally they break routine to climb clumsily up the bank to a favored backyard to beg for food. It is amusing to watch them scramble and fight for scraps of bread, then waddle away in a long, unwieldy line as they head back for the water. There, all trace of their awkwardness gone, they sail swiftly away.

The songbirds are nesting now, all of their energy directed at raising a family. A barn swallow darts in and out of the barn loft, intent on family business. There is a blur of crimson as a Carolina redbird settles near a flock of indigo buntings. The male bunting preens his brilliant blue feathers while his mousy brown wife watches. I heard my first whippoorwill of the spring last night, notes of pure silver floating across the twilight air. It makes me know that spring is really here.

Our verdant land glows with patches of bright color as May flowers continue to bloom. Patches of wild irises, delicate as any hothouse orchid, gleam bluely on the roadbank. Wild geraniums, in a lovely shade of lavender, bloom in clumps along the creek bank and in other rich places. The first wild asters appear, varying in color from white to pale shades of pink and purple. Wild azalea, which we call honeysuckle, with their splashy colors of yellow, orange, light and dark pink, is coming out in woodlots and hillsides. The rhododendron will soon burst into beauty as the clusters of pinkish-white, cup-shaped flowers appear. We always called this "big laurel," and its appearance when I was small meant our family reunion was very near. We looked forward to this gathering with great eagerness from year to year. We met with dozens of cousins, heaps of aunts and uncles, and had more good food than any young tummy could hold. When we were older, we would go down on Big Laurel Creek and swim all afternoon. Those really were the good old days.

Twilight trails dark, warm fingers across our

land and enfolds the hills in shadow. The last glimmer of the departing day shines on the horizon as night softly approaches. The strident song of the birds has dwindled down to a muted twitter, and the deepening silence is broken by the sleepy "quirr" of a tree frog. The air is warm and balmy, and the creak of the porch swing blends pleasantly with the night sounds. From across the creek comes the sudden sweet piercing call of the whippoorwill, and faintly from the woods comes an answering call.

This is truly the best part of the day, with all the chores done and there is time to relax in the porch swing. The grandchildren are beginning to run down too, and like the songbirds, their excited talk is dying away to sleepy murmurs. They have had a long, hard day. First they played in the creek, and then it was just a matter of time until the trio of three-year-olds (Luke, Abigail and Jessica) were in swimming. They didn't really plan to go skinny-dipping, but they got their clothes wet and it was the logical thing to take them off. They were having a marvelous time until their horrified mommies caught up with them. Luke then worked long and hard on a cabin. He must have pounded at least 150 new roofing nails in one little board, trying to fasten it to the garage. (His grandfather was somewhat less than impressed.) Then he trekked up and down the hill to the hog pen, with his faithful entourage — Jessica and Abigail — following him. There he spent hours tearing down an old gate. When he finally got it down in the yard, it fell to pieces. Hot and sweating, he gave up the project — I thought.

There are so many wonderful things to do this time of year. There are crawdabs to catch, holes to dig, trees to climb, and a troop of cousins to join in the fun. I remember how we loved long summer evenings when I was a kid. We would play tag, "stink" base, and hide and seek until darkness drove us home. Weary, but happy, we would often fall asleep during Daddy's nightly prayer. The boys would be sound asleep on their knees, and would have to be roused up and pointed toward the right bed. Even then, they would sometimes circle back and fall down on the couch. I sometimes wonder how Mom ever got all of us bedded down.

The Clay Free Press
May 30, 1984

School will soon be out, and how eagerly we used to look forward to the long days of summer vacation. It seemed that the summer stretched out endless before us, long inviting days of play. We had the woods to choose from, trees to climb, numerous playhouses, the creek to catch fish and crawdabs, and the barn to climb and romp in. We played long games of "Anthony Over," only we called it "Andy Over." It has been years since I've heard the call of "Andy Over." Kids don't seem to play the same games that we enjoyed so much. I can still hear the cry, "Bushel of wheat, bushel of rye, who's not ready, holler I! Bushel of wheat, bushel of clover, who's not ready, can't hide over!" The lightning bugs twinkled while we scurried from hiding place to hiding place. Alas, yesterday's summer is gone, like our childhood . . . much too soon.

The honeysuckle is blooming on the banks of Clay. It has always bloomed at graduation time; its sweet, clinging scent reminiscent of marching graduates, caps and gowns, and diplomas. The smell of honeysuckle has always loosed a flood of memories of my own graduation, bringing back the excitement of that time. There was a sadness in knowing that a stage of my life was forever gone, and a quivery feeling of standing on the brink of adulthood. High school graduation has always been a mixture of tears, laughter and memories.

There was that same lump-throat feeling when our first one graduated from high school. We watched him march across the stage to receive his diploma, grim and determined, and we felt strongly the milestone in our lives. We have seen all six of our children go through this process (one gave the valedictory address) with the feeling they were leaving the nest, one by one. When the last one made this step, there was a special pang for her, and for us.

The scent of honeysuckle has a new meaning for me now. It was the day after Memorial Day when Daddy was admitted to the hospital for vascular surgery. He went into the hospital, our old familiar Dad, and before the day was over a massive stroke reduced him to a broken shell of a man. I remember well the day of the surgery. We went down very early to see him before the pre-operative procedures began to take effect. He was laughing and joking as usual. His orderly was a sad-faced black man, and Daddy told him, "You look like you ate a sour pickle." The man's wrinkled face dissolved into laughter, and he began teasing Daddy. It was the last normal day of his life. It is strange how one day can change the lives of a whole family.

Daddy lived three years after that, a helpless and pitiful man. God, in His tender love and mercy, took him to a place where flowers are far sweeter than the honeysuckle grow. The Lord has comforted our hearts, and the memories that Daddy left behind are sweet.

Our pastor preached a message some time ago

about the changes that time has wrought. He stated that nothing ever remains the same in this life, and it is true that our life is just a series of mileposts. Death is a part of living, and if time lasts, it will come to all of us. Just like the high school graduates, we hover from time to time on the threshold of another stage of our lives, until we come to the final one. The most important thing in our lives is to know that we can stand before God uncondemned. Just like Daddy, I want to be ready when my time comes.

It is graduation and honeysuckle time again. It is also Memorial Day and remembering time again. The bittersweet fragrance wrenches my heart, and I remember Daddy.

Clay Free Press
June 2, 1982
Clay Herald
May 20, 1991

I can never remember a time when I didn't love Mary Ellen — or a time when I was angry with her.

I was five years old when she was born, but I can't remember her as a tiny baby. One memory stands out clearly in my mind, probably the earliest one I have of her. I was seven years old, and we lived at Davis Creek in Kanawha County at the time. She was a couple of years old, and I was carrying her on my back across the bottom below the house when suddenly such a rush of love for her flowed over me that almost fifty years later it is vivid in my mind. The bond of love is stronger between us now than then.

Daddy always called her "his baby," not because he made any difference in his love for any of us, but because he had to take over feeding her when she was five months old. Mom came down with a severe case of quinsy, a serious throat infection that necessitated weaning her. She wouldn't take a bottle, so Daddy had to feed her milk from a cup. She always tagged after him; even when he went out to build fence or work on the car, she would be a step or two behind him carrying a hammer or a screwdriver. I see her now, her face pink with exertion, and tiny drops of sweat beading her nose. She wore her hair in two pigtails, but somehow one of them invariably came loose and hung over her shoulder in kinky waves.

Mary Ellen would never fuss with the rest of us. In a family our size, there was generally a squabble going on between some of us, but she never joined in. I remember trying to provoke her a few times, but she simply wouldn't quarrel. We washed dishes in big metal dishpans, and I would drop the plates heavily to splash her. She would never say a word. On the other hand, Larry and I fought like cats and dogs.

She was the most fun to play with. We had a favorite little cove we called Sleepy Holler, and we spent much time there during the spring and summer. It was an enchanted place to us, thickly sprinkled with violets; pale blue ones with a long hooked spur, delicate white ones with the sweet fragrance that grew in the crevices of the rocks, white ones veined with purple, and dense patches of the common blue ones. Here the sweet-scented ferns grew in profusion, and lavender wild irises lent an exotic touch. It was barely out of sight of our house (but not out of hearing if we were called), and was a secluded little nook that was our own private world. A fallen log spanned the narrow ravine, and we played under it and on it. I wish every child could have a Sleepy Holler, and we adults need one many times to get away from the pressures of the world.

And so we grew up together, roaming the woods,

wading in the creek, and letting our imaginations run free. We got the idea that the Momma sow had dug her piglets out of the leaves, and we spent many unfruitful days digging diligently in the dry leaves for babies. How we longed to find a tiny newborn baby of our very own! We made fairy houses in the banks along the "little road," and although we knew better, it was such fun to pretend that fairies lived in them. We made miniature furniture out of acorn caps and penny match boxes, lined with a fuzzy mullein leaf. I would sneak and pin a shiny button on the fairy house wall, and tell Mary Ellen that the fairies did it while she was asleep.

We made playhouses in the barn, in the corn crib, and all over the woods. I remember when Mary Ellen and her friend Janice cleaned out a chicken house and made a playhouse in it. Our main ambition was to grow up and "be mommies" and have families.

Time passed so swiftly and soon we were both plunged into the serious but happy business of making homes, caring for a husband, and having babies. She became the same kind of wife and mother as she had been a little girl: serious and loving, dedicated and caring. She had three boys in succession, and her fourth baby was another boy that only lived an hour or so. Her faith in the Lord grew as the years went by, and she seemed to have a special feeling for young people. Her Sunday School class of teenage boys and girls could sense her concern and compassion, and the burden she carried for their souls.

But it wasn't just young people that she cared for. Mary Ellen has the peculiar talent of knowing just how to make the thoughtful gesture or say the right word when a person needs it most. Sick neighbors see her coming with a cooker of homemade soup, or a

48

fresh-baked cake, and always that earnest prayer
offered for them. When there is a need, Mary Ellen
can be counted on to be right there to offer assistance
and bolster faith.

Only the Lord knows how many times that her
arm of comfort has buoyed me up, the scripture verses
that were written and slipped into my hand, and the
whispered "I love you." It was the knowledge that she
really cared. It is not just because she is family that
I feel this way, but everyone who has just had their
paths to cross with Mary Ellen's has come away
rewarded and richer for the experience.

I had to stand back in awe as I saw her beloved
Savior lead her through the heaviest trial of her life —
the sudden, tragic death of her own teenage son,
David. I saw Jesus reflected through her love and
faith, and her increased burden for souls. It was
amazing to see her offer comfort to those who came to
comfort her, and to witness her unbounded faith in the
midst of the storm.

Mary Ellen is truly a child of God worth
knowing. I am humbly grateful to be her sister.
Clay Free Press
April 25, 1984

The first daisies of the year have appeared, and
as I picked and sniffed the slightly doggy smell of one,
I was immediately transported back to the hot summer
days of my childhood, with the playhouse in the
corncrib, and mud stirred up in tin cans. Remember
the one-piece zinc lids that we used to use for
canning? They had a glass liner that you could pound
out with a rock, and they made beautiful plates for a
little girl's playhouse. We spent many a summer day
making mud pies and cakes, decorated with pink and

red rambler roses.

It seems that today's children don't play the way we once did. It's quite rare to see a little girl making mud pies, and the woods no longer ring with the cries of little boys playing cowboys and Indians. I was sixteen years old before I quit playing "playhouse." Mary Ellen, Margaret Ann, and I had a playhouse up in the woods behind "Uncle" Clarence's house, when we were invaded by Billy Brown and Lawrence Parks. It so happened that I was sweet on Lawrence's brother Owen at the time. That ended my playhouse days.

Perhaps it was a more innocent age that we grew up in; certainly it was more unworldly. I look back on those days with a bittersweet sadness; days that can never be again — like my youth, gone too soon. But sometimes when the burdens get heavy, and the adult load is too much to bear, I can almost say with the poet, "Backward, turn backward, O time in your flight, Make me a child again just for tonight."

Clay Free Press
May 25, 1983

A GREEN AND GROWING TIME

With scarcely a ripple, spring drifts quietly into summer, with hot, steamy days and cool, comfortable nights. Roses spread their riotous beauty all around, while the common daisy, in more modest array, dots the countryside. The greenish-white lace appears on the elderberry bushes, and the hard, green blackberries form on the blackberry vines. Little boys scour the creek here, tadpoling and crawdabbing. The songbirds still raise their medley of joyous music at daybreak, but it soon dies away as they go about their more serious business of feeding their ever-hungry young. Criss leaves the feed room door open to the birds (and chipmunks), and a mourning dove, or rain crow, has been paying us an evening visit for the past week. With his slate gray suit and snowy white vest, he looks like a visiting dignitary paying a call on the local peasants.

The weather has been perfect for haying, and the farmers have been busy putting up hay. To me, nothing typifies summer on the farm more than the smell of sweet clover drying in the sun. The gardens need a little more rain, which the Lord will send in due season. The days go by in placid fashion, with most of the farm animals busy caring for their young. The old mother hen clucks to her brood of fluffy baby chickens as she teaches them to scratch for their food. Their tiny feet look quite comical as they imitate their mother, scratching industriously. Another setting hen hovers over her nest of eggs, patiently waiting for them to hatch. The earth is full of new life and the joy of living.

The children love these long summer evenings when they can play until their mothers call them home at bedtime. As I watch my grandchildren romp and play in the yard, I am reminded of the games we used to play at twilight. It has been years since I heard

children playing the old games. Patty remarks that
she would like to teach her children the same games
that they played, as they will soon be forgotten.

Do you remember playing, "Here we come,
Where are you from? Pretty girl station. What's your
trade? Lemonade. What's your initials? Get to work
and show us something." Then we played and sang,
"My chickie, my chickie, my craney, my crow, Went to
the well, To wash his big toe, When he got back, His
black hen was gone, What time is it, old witch?" I'm
sure many of you remember playing Old Bloody
Butcher, and chanting, "Who's going around my house
this dark, stormy night? "Old Bloody Butcher!"

We played a homemade game of "Old Witch" on
the Virginia Gas and Oil Company office porch, that
lasted for hours. It was a long porch that ran around
three sides of the tool house and office, and was made
for playing games. It was only after I was grown that
I realized what pests we must have been to the men
who worked there. I remember one man in particular,
whom we called "The Boss," by the name of Kester
Graham. That man surely fulfilled the scripture in
James 1:19 that says, "Let every man be swift to hear,
slow to speak, slow to wrath." In all my growing up
years I can't recall one time that he ever spoke a harsh
word to us. He was unfailingly kind to us, even at the
height of our rowdy games when he was doing his
paperwork.

The porch, which we called the "Virginia office"
is torn down and gone now. It was a favorite place to
play for all the neighborhood kids. We could skin the
cat on the iron pipes that arched over the gates, and
swing on the metal cable that encircled the yard. It
was a good place just to sit and talk at evening.

When we were older, we played "ring games."
These consisted of singing and skipping in a circle,

and we played them at all our parties. We played Miss Molly Brown, singing, "Oh, here comes Miss Molly Brown, Show me the way to London town, Stand you here, Stand you there, 'Til you hear the watchman cry." That one must surely have come over on the Mayflower. Then we sang lustily, "Go in and out the window," and "Four in the boat and the tide rolls high." Many of these games were played by Mom's generation, and were handed on down to us. Mom played "Skip to my Lou" and "The Old Dusty Miller." I hate to see them die out, as they surely will. They belong to an older generation, and I guess I do too.

Still, sometimes when the twilight falls, and the scent of honeysuckle is strong in the air, I can sense the "dear, dead days beyond recall." I again see Avis June and Charlie, Peggy Ann and Billy, Mabel Irene and Gerald, Betty Marie and Owen, Jeuell Beth and Alen Wayne, and Donald Ray (some of them forever gone) and faintly I can hear singing, "There goes a bluebird through the window, old Virginia style..."

Clay Free Press
June 22, 1983

The lighting bugs twinkle here and there in the gathering dusk tonight, and there is the far-off cry of the whippoorwill. I remember hundreds of summer nights like this, long ago evenings when we would play the old, old games.

I catch myself singing an old song out of the past: "Twilight is stealing over the sea, shadows are falling dark on the lee. Borne on the night winds, voices of yore, come from that far-off shore." It seems I can hear them tonight, those voices of yore, calling: "Bushel of wheat, bushel of rye, who's not ready, holler I!" There is a mad scramble to hide between the stock tanks and behind the compression station before the final call comes, "Bushel of wheat, bushel of clover, who's not ready, can't hide over — I'm coming!"

I have seen him everywhere today. While I worked in the garden, I saw his old house and yard with the big box elder in it. He stepped off the back porch, copper-colored hair and freckles, with the same engaging grin as of old. It seemed he was never still, but always busy on some project or another. He played the childhood games with the same vigor and intensity, and was always ready for a new adventure.

He was two years older than I, and was the boy who grew up next door. There is a close kinship between children who grow up together, and bonds forged that last a lifetime. He was like an older brother or a close cousin, and I loved him in that fashion. He was the youngest in his family, while I was the oldest of seven. He once called me "the old woman who lived in a shoe" because of the retinue of small children who always tagged after us. But one of my younger sisters recalls how good he was to "us little ones," so he really didn't mind. Along with Coda, who also lived in sight, and Reva and Margaret Ann, we were a core of neighborhood children who played together all through the years. Sometimes we were joined by Jeuell Beth and Janice, who lived on up in the holler, for the evening games together.

All through the long days of childhood we played, when the summer days stretched out into infinity and it seemed we would always be young. We played in the barn, which was sometimes a pirate ship on the high seas, and at other times a secret clubhouse. We climbed on his father's garage roof and picked off the bitter Russet apples from the tree that grew beside it. We gorged on green apples from the trees up in the bottom, and suffered the green apple bellyache together. In the winter when it was too cold to play outside, we would act out comic strip characters: the Katzenjammer Kids with Cap'n and Mama, and the two little hellions, Hans and Fritz. We caught minnows, crawdabs, and pennywinkles in the creek and played "Old Witch" on the Virginia office porch for hours on end.

Childhood came to an end, and high school graduation brought a parting of the ways. "Pug" joined the Air Force, where in time he became a major. He married a Texas girl; they had four children and made Texas their home. My life in the hills continued in the age-old pattern, while his was a world apart.

We corresponded through the years, by letter and telephone, and the sense of kinship remained. He had not been home for many years, and had been in declining health, when he began expressing a desire to come home "one more time." He asked wistfully if the big apple trees were still up in the bottom, and I had to tell him that they had been gone for years. "It looks different, Pug," I told him. There is a house and a couple of trailers where we once climbed the apple trees, although I see them plainly in memory.

This spring, his plans grew more concrete to make a visit home. "I want my children to see where I grew up," he explained in a phone call. He was making plans to come home this fall.

Last week, I got an excited call from him. "I'm coming home the week of the Fourth," he told me. His wife, son, daughter-in-law, and two grandchildren were coming with him. "I want to see you, and the old home place," he continued. As soon as he hung up, I called his sister in St. Albans and invited her and her husband to come up that day also. I planned to cook him a real country meal, with fresh half-runner beans and other things. Mom had a package of real home-cured dried apples, and I wanted to make him a dried apple pie — a favorite of his childhood.

Friday evening I received an unexpected phone call. Alen Wayne had passed away that morning. With a smile on his face, he had gone home for the last time.

The lonely quirr of a tree frog is heard in the deepening darkness, and my heart is sad as I remember the last words to the song:

"Far away, beyond the starlit skies, where the love light never, never dies / Gleameth a mansion, filled with delight, sweet happy home is so bright."

The Charleston Gazette
July 10, 1992

June has glided in softly, bringing graduation, roses, and blushing brides. Criss and I sat in the bleachers and watched Crystal receive her eighth grade diploma. As the graduating class marched in, it hit me suddenly that this is our last one to go through this ceremony. The old familiar lump rose up in my throat and forced helpless tears and I wanted to cry out, "No, she's not old enough to be doing this — just last week I held her in my arms and brushed the baby curls out of her eyes. And wasn't it only yesterday that the pastor's wife and I enrolled her and Shelly in kindergarten?" (There were some swallowed-back tears that day, only I'm afraid it was the mothers' — Crystal and Shelly never looked back.) Perhaps that is significant in our relationship; while I cry, Crystal never looks back.

Grandma O'Dell's "graveyard rose" is in full bloom; big, soft, fragile roses that put out a heavenly fragrance. It has blossomed every year since I can remember. The old fashioned rambler roses are spilling their compact little blossoms over fence and roadbank. The common daisy brightens every nook and corner with its bright-eyed, cheerful bloom.

June was a perfect time for our mock weddings. It didn't take much to have one — just an old curtain for a bridal gown, and a willing groom. We always had an ample supply of brides, but grooms were a little harder to come by. I can remember one wedding we had all planned out, and my brother Larry reluctantly agreed to play the groom to Janice Carole. I made a clay-mud wedding cake, decorated with pink and red rambler roses, and was about to perform the ceremony. (I was always the minister — as the oldest, I got to boss the operation.) At the last minute, Larry got cantankerous and backed out. I threw a terrible tantrum and stomped the wedding cake, and in the face of my awesome wrath, Larry ran off and wouldn't play with us the rest of the day.

Daisies are so much a part of summer when you are growing up. I don't see how anyone could ever have a playhouse without them. They make a perfect fried egg, sunnyside up, and their crumbled centers have garnished many a playhouse salad. Along with the "beans" from the redbud tree, we served plenty of make believe meals. We spent the biggest part of our summer "playing house". It is a rare thing to see little girls now making playhouses.

We had special playhouses for special uses. Some we built in the woods, with lovely moss carpets and rooms marked off by sticks. Some we used just for "show" and it was forbidden to mix mud in them or dirty them in any way. But the ones we enjoyed the most were made on the big rock across the creek. There was a seam of gray clay mud close by, plenty of water to mix and stir in it, and we made mud pies and cakes by the hour. Our bridal cakes in June were works of art, decorated liberally with daisies and the rambler roses that grew all over the side of the house and down over the creekbank itself. Sometimes I get the urge to make mud pies just one more time, and if I take the granddaughters, I could probably get by with it.

Clay Free Press
June 6, 1984

Jessica is building a playhouse in the old hog house.

It is not as bad as it sounds; it has been years since we kept any animals in it, and it has been used for playhouses many times in the summer since then. Matthew and his friend Jeff made a cozy clubhouse in it one time, covering it with indoor-outdoor carpet and installing a wood cookstove made from a fifty-five gallon metal drum. It got too cozy that time, as the roof caught fire from their makeshift stovepipe and they hastily vacated the premises. The grandkids have played there from year to year, and this spring Jessica is moving in.

I see her carrying cherished items up the bank; cracked cups and discarded kitchenware, plus an old ice chest to use as a refrigerator. Her eyes lit up when I found a discarded canister set in the cellar, and a coffeemaker that no longer works. Her long, brown braids bob up and down, and beads of sweat pop out on her upper lip as she toils up and down the hill in the sunshine. I remember the special feeling that a playhouse brings.

We built playhouses all over these hills, in the woods, and in the barn. But the playhouse that I loved best was in the old corncrib. It was built long and narrow; high off the ground so that you had to climb up and crawl in the door. The ceiling was so low that you couldn't stand upright, even as a young'en. The odor of dry corn was permanently imbedded in it, no matter how much you cleaned and swept. When Daddy cleaned it out in the spring, he always uncovered at least one nest of baby mice which we would beg to keep. They were so cute, with their tiny, hairless bodies and tummies so transparent that you could see the blood pumping through their veins. We would hold the warm, pink, helpless bodies in our hands and plead for their lives. Daddy would explain that baby mice would eventually grow up to become adult mice, which were dirty and destructive. We would usually sneak one little fellow out and try to raise him in a match box lined with cotton. An eye dropper of warm milk provided his diet, and we would feed and mother our "baby" for two or three days with the inevitable results — waking up to find him cold and stiff. Then we would shed a few bitter tears and bury him, matchbox and all, with pomp and ceremony.

The corncrib was big enough to make a bed in one corner, which we fashioned from an old quilt and some cushions. We really played in our playhouse, too; mixing mud and pokeberries to make cakes and pies.

A rag spread over a cardboard box made a table, and we picked wild flowers for "flower pots" — not arrangements or bouquets. There our homemaking "skills" were developed, and our maternal instincts were nurtured. Mary Ellen and I were always "Mommies" and Jeannie and Susie were our "babies." Mary Ellen claimed Susie, and Jeannie was mine. (This carried over to practical matters at home, as it was our responsibility to get each "baby" ready for bed, and we shared a bed with our own special charge. With seven children born in twelve years, Mom needed all the help she could get. And we loved it — we had two double beds in one bedroom, and there we slept. The ties it forged among four sisters are tightly knit today.)

The most pleasant times in our corncrib playhouse was when it was raining. There, shut up in our own private world, dry and cozy, we spent many happy hours. It seemed so real. The boys would sometimes play with us, but they weren't very satisfactory playmates. They would play for a while, then get bored and want to roughhouse, or they would take off to the woods. I guess that is where we learned our roles in life — we "mommies" stayed home and kept house, while the "daddies" went out and climbed trees.

I believe every little girl needs a play house. I still find myself, when walking through the woods, eyeing a nice, flat rock and thinking about playhouse possibilities. That must be the reason I like to camp out so well — it's almost like playing house again.

There goes Jessica and Luke back to the hog house, trailed by Joseph. Luke is still young enough not to be embarrassed to play "daddy" and Joseph makes a cooperative "baby". I can hear them talking, "Let's pretend like you're the mommy, and I'll be the daddy and I'll go to work while you stay here and take care of the baby . . . "

Almost all we read in the newspapers is bad news — pollution, crime, violence, threat of nuclear war, graft, extortion, divorce, broken homes — and on and on. But have hope.

Jessica is building a playhouse.
The Clay Herald
April 24, 1989

I just went out to inspect the grapevines and

found one of Criss' young cherry trees, which was finally beginning to grow, chopped down to the ground. There was evidence scattered everywhere (belonging to Criss) a handful of nails, two claw hammers, and a lean-to cabin composed of two pieces of paneling leaned up against the shop. (Luke hadn't abandoned his cabin project — just postponed it.) Inside the cabin, I found the top of a lazy Susan holding some dishes from the playhouse, a stool, and a pair of bathroom scales — the necessities of life, I suppose. I am not saying who did it, but I have a sneaking suspicion that it wasn't George Washington.

Our pastor counsels that we should not make sissies out of our little boys, but let them play and get dirty. Luke really lives up to the message. Patty stopped here after a visit to Jackson County, and Luke got out of the car with the blackest face I've ever seen. He had a baby 'possum curled up on his head and clinging to his hair. "It thinks I'm his mommy," he told me proudly. I don't think anyone will ever mistake Luke for a girl — a varmint, maybe. Adrian is following in his footsteps. He already has a pet mud puddle that he gravitates to every day. At thirteen months, he rides a go-cart with his older brothers, his chestnut burr hair sticking straight up.

My baby brother, Ronnie, had a penchant for mud puddles also when he was little. We had a resident puddle close to the yard, and Ronnie spent his younger days growing up in it. I don't think we would have recognized him without his coating of mud.

Mom used to catch the rain water that poured off the house in washtubs to do laundry. I can still hear the old refrain, "Ronnie's in your wash water!" and we'd find him washing his muddy little body in her clean wash water. He would look up with an angelic smile, and it was hard to punish him. He still

practices that angelic smile, but I don't think it gets
him very far now.

The Clay Free Press
May 30, 1984

We had pretend church services, and I
remember one baptismal service in particular. The
creek was much cleaner when I was a kid, and
virtually free of broken glass. It had rained and raised
the creek, and although it was slightly muddy, it was
warm and just right for playing and splashing. We
played for awhile, and then decided to have a
baptizing. We were having a wonderful time, running
the banks and shouting, "Hallelujah!" and "Glory!" and
dipping each candidate under the muddy water, when
the wrath of God appeared in the form of Mom. She
was totally scandalized. "I could hear you shouting all
the way over to the house," she snapped the words
out. "What will the neighbors think?" She always said
that, and I don't know what difference it made because
the neighbor's children were usually right in the
middle of our escapades — in fact, we had just
baptized some of them. She told us we were being
sacrilegious, but we weren't really. We were just
imitating the things we had seen our parents do. I was
reminded of that instance when I caught some of our
grandchildren having a similar service in the middle of
our bed. I started to say something when my sister
defended them. "They are just doing the things they
see us do," she said. "What other kind of life do they
know?"

I got to thinking of how very much our children
and grandchildren do imitate the very life we live. We
ought to make straight paths for our feet, because

64

many little feet are following our footsteps.
The Clay Free Press
June 9, 1982

I still see him everywhere.
It has been almost 13 years since he went away, but it seems like yesterday that he walked these hills . . . alive and vital. It is hard to believe that he is really gone. I am reconciled to his going — it's just that I miss him so much.

I never hear a whippoorwill that I don't think of him. He loved their clear call at dusk, and the answering echoes from the opposite hill as other whippoorwills took up the call. Every time I see a spectacular sunset, I find myself wishing he could share it. So many times he would come into the house to call me outside to see the sun going down in all its splendor. He wanted all of us to witness the glory of a rainbow. We would stand in the misting rain and lift our eyes toward Pilot Knob to see the arching rainbow reaching from mountain to mountain. "There's a pot of gold at the end of it," he would say with a twinkle in his eye. Then on a more serious note he would always remind us that the rainbow is God's promise to us that He would never again destroy the earth with water.

So many, many things remind me of him. The changing of the seasons was a source of delight to him. The coming of spring was greatly anticipated and he never lost a childlike wonder at the marvel of God's creation. He loved autumn, too, although many times he would remark that it was a "sad time." He taught us to love and appreciate the handiwork of God, from the tiniest wild flower to the tall, towering oak in the forest. We learned a reverence for life as we stood on tiptoe and gingerly looked at the tiny, naked birds in their nest. We held our breath, because he told us that if we breathed on them, the ants would eat them. We would never dare poke an inquisitive finger at them if our breath did so much damage.

We learned to love nature just as he did through the many fishing and camping trips. The tangy smell of wood smoke on a cool spring morning, the rippling rush of the trout stream, the tantalizing fragrance of bacon and eggs as Mom cooked breakfast over an open fire — we shared in all of these. I still see him there.

How many times have I looked up the hill toward the Ball Diamond and half expected to see him striding down the path! He has a scythe over his shoulder, and his faded blue chambray shirt is drenched in perspiration; his face flushed and red with his exertions.

I recall one time when he was mowing on the hill, and his grandson David Paul, who was about four then, had accompanied him to the meadow. Daddy had a whet rock that he used to sharpen his scythe, and he admonished David "not to touch it — it is very easy to break." David listened with interest, and as soon as Daddy's back was turned, he picked it up, whacked it on a rock, and broke it into three pieces. When Daddy turned around, David told him with a grin, "Look, Poppy, now you've got three!" I think Daddy spanked him, but had to laugh about it later when he related the episode.

There is a spot down in the woods coming down the hill from the Ball Diamond where Daddy's presence is almost tangible. A big rock overshadows a small spring there in that secluded spot, and that is where he had his secret place of prayer. Every day he made a pilgrimage there to commune with the Father that he loved so much. He would come back to the house, his face shining and happy, and we would know where he had been. I was down there just a few days ago in the peaceful solitude, and his presence seemed to linger there still. I whispered, "Daddy?", but of course there was no answer except the rustle of leaves above my head and a lone bird that sang somewhere close in the underbrush.

Someone wrote to me once and asked why I didn't tell the truth about Daddy — how he was a scoundrel in his younger days, and made moonshine which he also imbibed. All I know are some humorous family anecdotes of his driving his Model-T Ford with his eyes shut (I am sure he was three sheets in the wind) and wiping out part of Clarence Brown's fence. Also he once placed his gum boots in the middle of the floor, stood on the bed, and attempted to jump into them. Isn't it wonderful that God can take a life that is deep in sin and make a complete change? When He takes our sins away, He remembers them no more. People may remember but that doesn't matter. I don't think many of us would want our past lives held up to public scrutiny — how many of us would pass with flying colors? I am thankful that my memories of Daddy are of a good, deeply spiritual man who lived a life before his children that carries an impact yet today.

I see him in our church services. Sometimes when the choir gets up to sing, I visualize him sitting on the second pew where he usually sat. He has on the blue plaid sports coat that was his favorite, and his face is beaming. I once was asked what he used on his face that made it so shiny — it was merely the reflection of the happiness in his soul. When the choir sings "I Love Him," I can see Daddy's radiant smile and can almost reach out and touch him . . .

On this Father's Day, I am so thankful for Daddy's greatest legacy to us; a deep and abiding faith in our Savior. The most important duty that any father has is to bring up his children in the right way. The charge was given long ago, and is just as necessary today. Deut. 6:4-7 says, "Hear, O Israel, the Lord our God is one Lord: And thou shalt love the Lord thy God with all thine heart, and with all thy soul, and with all thy might. And these words, which I command you this day, shall be in thine heart: and thou shalt teach them diligently to thy children."

The Clay Free Press
June 19, 1985

Dear Daddy:

How my heart longs to spend just one more day with you! I would get up very early in order to savor every precious moment, and I know just where I would choose to go — back down on Big Laurel Creek to the old home place where I was born. (Daddy, I have regretted bitterly that I didn't go that fall when you asked me to go and spend the day with you. I stupidly thought that I had too much to do, and Patty went instead. She has told me many times since that she wouldn't take a million dollars for that golden autumn day that she spent with you. It was the last fall before your stroke. How could I have been so blind to what is important?)

We would explore the now lonely farm, and you would show me where the old house, now long gone, once stood. A straggly japonica bush is the only evidence that people once lived and loved, laughed and cried, were born and died there. You would show me where Grandpa Huge once had his corn fields, and point out the holes of water where you and Mom snared the big suckers that abounded in the creek then. You would tell me how poor but happy you and

Mom were as newlyweds, and I know you would show
me the place where you dug out the groundhog while
Mom watched with me in her arms. I can hear you
laughing as you recall how the rock flew and hit me in
the nose, and how Mom cried along with me because
she thought I was killed.

Daddy, I have so many things to tell you. How
you would enjoy these great-grandchildren and how
they would love you! I can see you rocking Adrian and
singing, "Here comes Adrian with a snigger and a grin,
Groundhog grease all over his chin!" I would tell you
about Kevin living for the Lord and singing his praises,
and how Freddie is so faithful. I would tell you about
losing David Paul, how the grief cuts and our hearts
ache.

I think that is what I have missed most about
you, Daddy — not being able to tell you everything,
and knowing that you would understand. But there
are some things I am glad you have been spared,
although at one time I ached to throw myself into your
arms and sob out my sorrow and heartache. I am
learning to lean more and more upon the Lord. Not
only can I tell Him everything and He understands, but
He also has the power to change the situation. I am so
thankful for the understanding you showed as an
earthly father, that I might better understand the care
and compassion of a Heavenly Father. What better
way can we learn than by having a godly father who is
a living example of abiding faith in God?

The day would end all too soon, Daddy. We
would have to part for now, and I would kiss you and
say, "Good-bye, Daddy, I love you." I know what your
answer would be, that loving phrase that I have heard
all my life and ache to hear again, "Good-bye, Alyce

Faye, I love you too."

Have you ever wondered what Emily Post would do in certain situations? Several years ago my brother Mark was working as a pipefitter at the Beckley VA Hospital. At noon a crew of men were sitting in the corridor peacefully eating their lunch, when a sudden sneeze exploded, and an object, like a bird or a bat, flew past Mark's face. He automatically stuck out his hand and batted it to the floor. The old man next to him looked disbelievingly at his shattered dentures on the floor, then at Mark who was by then wishing himself a thousand miles from there. (I don't know if the old man had finished his lunch or not. Let's hope that if he hadn't, that he didn't have celery or carrot sticks. There are a lot of things to be considered here. Was this a job-related accident? Would he be eligible for compensation? But I digress. . .)

Kids are another problem — sometimes you simply don't know what to do. My mother is at home recovering from surgery, and my daughter-in-law Phyllis and her four-year-old son Benji took her a bowl of fresh-baked cookies. Benji sat politely for about five seconds and then announced, "I want a cookie!" Embarrassed, Phyl told him,"Hush, Benji, we brought these cookies to Mom-Granny." Undaunted, Benji says more loudly, "But I want a cookie!" Phyl is getting red-faced. "Benji," she said firmly, "We have cookies at home." Of course Mom gave him a cookie, which he promptly devoured, and then another. Phyllis is quite shy, and easily embarrassed, so she put the bowl of cookies on a high shelf and went out on the porch with Mom and the baby. In a few minutes they heard a terrible crash, the bowl of cookies flew across the floor, crumbs shot under the storm door, with Benji in hot pursuit. He ate all of them, including the crumbs.

When Kevin was about Benji's age, we were on a telephone party line with a former neighbor, who tied up the line for hours on end. One day at a social function I found myself seated right beside her. "How do you do, Mrs. Blank?" I asked politely. I saw Kevin's ears pick up. Before I could stop him, he leaned across me and said, "Mrs. Blank, you talk on the telefoam all the time." I tried to crawl under the seat, but what could you say? I need a book of manners that covers these situations.

Jeff Braley killed a huge rattlesnake while he was motorcycle riding through Ash Camp this week, and brought it home to show his dad. His father inquired, "Where's its rattlers?" "I knocked them off," Jeff replied. "Well, where's its head?" his father persisted. "I knocked it off when I killed it," Jeff explained. His father was indignant. "You've ruint it; you've plumb ruint it," he told Jeff. Jeff said patiently, "Dad, how could you ruin a rattlesnake?"

The Clay Free Press
July 7, 1982

Midsummer has settled down on our hills and hollers with blistering hot days, and sticky, humid nights. Dog days have set in with a vengeance with resulting stagnant water, mold and mildew.

The little white blossoms are dropping from the elderberry bushes and the tiny green berries are beginning to form. The raspberries are ripe; black, dusky caps that melt in your mouth. Blackberries have turned bright red, although early reports indicate that the crop doesn't look too favorable. Picking blackberries used to be one of the highlights of summer when I was a kid.

Our upper pasture field was once a thriving blackberry patch, and we made daily pilgrimages there as long as the berries lasted. Only a country youngster can fully appreciate the labor involved in blackberry picking. You have to go early, before the sun rises in its searing heat, and at first it is cool and refreshing in the early morning. The weeds and underbrush are wet with the nighttime dew, and the air is fresh and reviving. The nutmeg- scented, pink wildflower is blooming, and the birds are singing their summer melody. Laden with water buckets and half bushel tubs, we climb the hill to the berry patch. The first hour is fun, and then the heat and the sweat-bees set in. It is a bedraggled bunch that emerges late in the day, arms brier-scratched and bleeding, fighting sweat-bees and chiggers, and mouths smeared purple with berries that were too ripe to put in the bucket. Ronnie nearly always managed to spill his bucket of berries on the way home (if not before) and would bring his offering to Mom covered with dirt, sticks and bits of moss. Still, it was about the only way we had to earn any money during the summer, for we could pick and sell berries after Mom got what she wanted to can and put away for the winter.

The summer before I started to high school, I picked and sold enough berries to order two pieces of corduroy material from the Sears catalog. Mom made me two long, straight skirts that touched the top of my anklets. Worn with saddle oxfords, I felt right in style. Not too long ago, one of my friends asked me if I remembered those corduroy skirts that I would jerk off the clothesline and wear — with never the pretense of

an iron. How could I forget?
The Clay Free Press
July 14, 1982

The sugar corn waves proud tassels in the air and the half runner beans hang full and green on the vines. Our country gardens are producing abundantly, and our days are filled with pickling, canning and freezing. It is the busiest time of the year for the country housewife, and it seems that we will never be able to cram all that work into a few short weeks. However the summer will soon be over and the fall days will be upon us.

These sweltering days makes me think of the old swimming hole of our childhood and the days we spent playing in the creek. We would spend hours catching crawdabs and the tiny shellfish that we called "penniwinkles." I haven't seen a penniwinkle for years. I wonder if they are gone from here? Mom always told us that the creek in dog days would make "fall sores" on our legs, and we usually had them. Remember the purple medicine (gentian violet) that we dabbed on our arms and legs? It was worth running the risk, though, when the days were hot and dry and the creek called to us.

Despite all the heat, there is still beauty all around us. We drove to Jackson County to visit baby sister Susie, and the roadbanks were lined with blue chicory as far as the eye could see. Interspersed were the bold black-eyed Susans and the delicate beauty of Queen Anne's lace. They seem to thrive in the hot sunlight. There are special joys of summertime — hot, buttered ears of sweet corn and ice cold watermelon eaten outside so that the sweet juice can run off your elbows and eyebrows. They're just as good now as

when I was a barefoot young'en.
                    The Clay Free Press
                    July 21, 1982

The fullness of summer is upon us with trees in full leaf and hot, droning days. Dawn brings the singing of the birds, rejoicing in another new day as the first golden rays of the sun finger the treetops. I love these tranquil summer days with their bright blue skies and long hours of hot sunshine. This morning the hills look clean and fresh-scrubbed after last night's thunderstorms that broke the heat wave. Raindrops sparkle on the roses, and the elderberries glisten black. It is so peaceful here in the hills in early morning and I feel a great sense of contentment fill my soul. Contentment is a wonderful thing; to be satisfied with who you are and where you are. I believe that true contentment comes only when you are at peace with God and man.

It will soon be time to harvest the elderberries for jelly, but you can also use the bloom. I tried a wild food recipe one time where you snipped the whole cluster of blossoms, then washed and drained it well. You dipped the whole cluster in a rich batter made of milk, flour and eggs and deep-fried them in oil. Dusted with powdered sugar, they were delicate and delicious. They also gave me the worst case of heartburn I'd had in a long time. I have always been fascinated with wild foods, and will try almost anything. I have stewed day lily buds and immature milkweed pods. I have always wanted to try fiddle-head ferns, but I am not sure which ones they are. We like the oyster mushrooms that grow on certain types of wood and look like gilled seafood. The sulphur, or chicken mushroom, is worth hunting.

Of all the jobs back in the good old days, hoeing corn was one of the worst. I spent three hours hoeing corn this week and remembered when we used to put the whole bottom in field corn. It would take us at least a week to hoe it, and the days grew long and hot. We hoed barefoot, and sand briers were a constant nuisance. About the time you got the sharp little boogers picked out, the sweat-bees would attack. If you began fighting them you were sure to get stung. You would anyway; they would crawl up under your clothes, or you would mash one under your armpit. I remember when Larry would get hot and thirsty, and cranky with sweat-bee stings, and begin hoeing recklessly. He would cut down the young corn and hill up the weeds until Daddy would take his hoe and relieve him for awhile. Daddy would say apologetically to me, "Some people just can't learn to hoe corn." I think some people just didn't like to hoc corn. It is a funny thing, now Larry has a beautiful garden.

There was nothing like the relief when the corn was "laid by" or hoed for the last time. We always finished in the upper corner of the garden where the two big apple trees grew. I would throw my hoe and lie down full length on the ground to get the kinks out of my back. But our corn patch was nothing compared to the fields of corn that my mother and her family had to hoe. They hoed for weeks and then hired out to the neighbors for fifty cents a day. Those were good old days?

I wonder if that wasn't why they raised a better generation of kids. You get a boy up at four-thirty and send him to the barn before breakfast to milk a couple of cows, and then to the cornfield after — when night came, he was ready for bed. I believe that the reason a lot of young people get into trouble now is because they don't have enough to do.

As the day draws to a close the grandchildren are running to and fro on the lawn catching lightning bugs to put in a glass jar. We are never lonesome around here. Luke is sporting a brand new haircut that he gave himself — "So Adrian can't pull my hair," he explains. Patty mourns, "I can't straighten it up — it's cut clear into the hide on one side!" Jessica holds her new baby brother and caresses him. She is so possessive. "He's your baby brother, but he's Benji's too," I admonish her. Her black eyes snap at me as she retorts, "He's a little bit Benji's, and a whole lot mine!"

The Clay Free Press
July 4, 1984

It had been a long time since I'd spent a whole day with one of the grandsons. At four years of age, Adrian is next to the youngest grandchild. A young man once described his sister to me, a big, strapping girl in her twenties, as the "babiest one" in the family.

Adrian's mother had to be gone for the day, so I had the pleasure of his company for an entire day. He is forty inches tall and weighs forty pounds. His mother describes him as square, and his grandfather calls him a fireplug. He is a short, sturdy little boy; a curious blend of old-man wisdom and baby-fat winsomeness. His engaging grin flashes silver from metal-capped front teeth. This is Adrian.

He arrived before breakfast with a bag of clothes he had packed by himself. We unloaded four pairs of pants, four shirts, two pairs of underwear, and a pair of boxer shorts — all for one day's visit. His grandpa laughed when I held up the tiny pair of boxer shorts. "They're my boxin' bloomers," he yelled as he spread his feet apart and assumed a typical boxer's stance, his fists doubled up in front of his face. With his short legs and stocky build, he resembles a miniature Japanese sumo wrestler more than he does a junior Joe Louis.

After a hearty breakfast of scrambled eggs, toast and tea, Adrian feels a little sleepy so he curls up on the couch and pops his thumb in his mouth. Immediately, the parrot perched on the piano above his head looks down and sets up an agitated screeching. Adrian listens for a few minutes, removes his thumb and says sleepily, "Mommaw, I know a good name for that bird — Chuckles!"

He wakes up from his nap, rested and ready to play. He tackles a large cardboard box with a hacksaw blade and fashions a post office. He claims all of the morning's junk mail and raids the wastebasket for yesterday's discards. (Any grandmother worth her salt does so have time to draw an American flag, letter a United States Post Office sign, make an OPEN/CLOSED sign, bandage a cut knuckle (from the hacksaw blade) kiss away a tear, hunt some old letters and steam off several used stamps, and visit the post office for mail many times.)

Adrian is such a happy youngster, and likes to make everyone feel good. (I love sardines in mustard sauce, so Adrian's father gift wraps me several tins each Christmas. This year as I unwrapped the usual offering, Adrian had his elbows propped on my knees watching intently. As the tins of sardines came into view, Adrian commented sweetly, "Just what you wanted, Mommaw — fish guts!")

Later I saw him poring over a sports magazine, the front cover depicting the survival of the fittest — a painting of a couple of weasels that had downed a grouse for their dinner. He looked up at me, his brown eyes shining, and said softly, "Oh, Mommaw, look at the squirrels hugging that bird!" I hate to see him grow up and shed that innocent outlook, gradually replaced by the cynicism that growing knowledge brings. No wonder that Jesus told us, "Verily I say unto you, except ye be converted, and become as little children, ye shall not enter into the kingdom of heaven."

However, Adrian is growing and expanding his horizons. His older brother, Aaron, helped him hold a BB gun and shoot a pesky mole that was tunneling through his other grandmother's yard. In relating the incident to her, he squared his shoulders and announced proudly, "Grammaw, I killed a wart!"

That day went fast, with the post office to attend and his helping me with my chores. He's at that delightful age where he is anxious to please, and willing to help with whatever you are doing. Too soon he will start kindergarten, and join the ranks of the other boys who have too many interests to spend a day with Mommaw.

The post office is packed up and carted away, his treasures are collected and gone, and his mother has taken him home. His artwork decorates the front of my refrigerator — art that only a grandmother can appreciate.

Yes, the day is over and gone — but there is a knock at my front door. It is Adrian, his lunch box packed and his BB gun over his shoulder, with an invitation to go hunting with him. Hmmm — I wonder if a four-year-old grandson and a fifty-two-year-old grandmother could bag some big game?

The Clay Herald
January 25, 1988

It seems that I write more about the grandsons

than I do the granddaughters — perhaps because there are so many little boys. The girls are much in evidence. Christina (Mike's), Abigail (Kevin's), and Jessica (Andy's) are growing like weeds; baby fat melting away into knobby knees under dresses that are constantly too short. They are like petunias this time of year — all angles and "sprangly" growth. Yet they bloom so well.

Chrissie looks like a perfect little lady, but appearances can be quite deceiving. With her ruffles and curls, she can be found more often perched on the limb of a tree, or hanging upside down by her legs, than sitting demurely on a chair. She has a robust laugh that contrasts oddly with her appearance, and she belts it out at unexpected times. She just came through surgery for the second time to correct a deviation of the septum. I have never seen a more co-operative patient than she was. She never made a whimper when she awakened from surgery, and did everything the nurses told her. (This, from the same little girl who went into hysterics the week before from a wasp sting, and had to be calmed down with a swat on the behind!) She woke up with her nose stuffed with packing and bandaged from upper lip to her eyelids. I told her she looked like the Cowardly Lion — all you could see were those green eyes gleaming. She is home now and doing fine.

Jessica really is ladylike. With her long brown braids and dark eyes, she looks angelic. Again, don't go by appearances. She can erupt like a volcano into a spitfire. She is a motherly soul, and makes an excellent baby sitter as she hovers over her baby brother Joseph. I believe she is going to inherit her mother's homemaking talents. Phyllis was cooking supper the other evening and stepped into the back room to put a load of clothes in the washer. She told

Jessica to watch the food on the stove — just to keep her occupied. Jessica put on an apron, pulled a chair close the kitchen stove, and climbed up with a tablespoon in her hand. Phyl had the washer and dryer both running, and failed to hear a knock on the door. Jessica, in her apron and carrying the spoon, invited the man in. She then climbed back on her chair and resumed her watch over the meal. When Phyl returned to the kitchen, she found an insurance salesman sitting at the table and watching Jessica in complete fascination. I don't think Phyl tried to explain.

Abigail is another story. She has been described as the "Little Iodine of Ovapa" — an apt title indeed. She is called Miriam by most of the family, but she will never be anything but Abigail to me. She looks a lot like her mama Sarah, with a dab of Grandpap Thad thrown in for good measure. She doesn't even pretend to be a lady. Her brother Josh calls her a "grubworm", as she loves mud puddles, fishing worms and crawdabs. She hates to have her hair combed, and can get her face dirty on the three minute drive to church. She is constantly on the move, and dogs my footsteps. Her heart's desire is to be a grandma like me.

There are only four months between her and Jessica, and they are bosom pals. As bosom pals often do, they clash occasionally (both being quite opinionated), and the hair and fingernails fly. In a few minutes they are reconciled, and playing house with their doll babies once again.

The grandsons have had a busy summer. Right now an orange spotted salamander looks at me as I type. He is safely ensconced in a glass jar, and is perched on a rock protruding out of the water. This is his day of freedom as Josh plans to turn him loose.

The boys have a great collection of living creatures. I called Patty last week and Luke answered the telephone. When I asked what he and Aaron were doing, he replied in an offhand manner, "Oh, we are catching bugs for Charlotte." By the time Patty got on the phone I was curious. "Who in the world is Charlotte?" I asked. "Oh, Mommy," she wailed, "The boys have caught a giant black spider about the size of a teacup and turned it loose in the house. They call it Charlotte, and are catching bugs for it!" I decided not to visit her that day.

Our friend Debbie took Patty's boys down to the creek to catch crawdabs. They had caught several and placed them in a bucket of water, when Debbie caught Luke pounding the contents with a stick. "Stop that, Lukie," she yelled. "You're killing the crawdabs." "I not killing them, Debbie," he replied sweetly. "I teaching them to fight!"

Luke yelled at his mother a few days ago and said, "Hey, Mommy, I need help but I know you won't help me when you see what I'm doing!" Naturally these words would galvanize any mother into action and she investigated immediately. She found him trying to tie a sewing thread on an ant, and bawled him out for being cruel. Quite reasonably, he explained, "I was just trying to hitch him up so he could pull something!" Hitch your wagon to an ant — what a title for a high school commencement speech.

The Clay Free Press
August 20, 1986

Our world is squeaky clean this morning, after yesterday's rain washed the dust away. Puffy white clouds create patches of light and shadow as they move swiftly across the blue sky, and the tender green leaves on the trees quiver in the wind. The hills are covered in green; the trees, underbrush and forest floor are all garbed in their summer wear. The evergreens sport velvety-soft new growth on the tips of their branches, and the white blooms on the cucumber trees look like candles in the woods.

Our grandchildren exult in the warming weather and greening outdoors. Evidence of their activity abounds. I opened the lid on a five-gallon plastic bucket on the back porch to be greeted by one bullfrog, one tree frog, and one spring peeper. I don't know who was the most surprised. I released them in the ditch, but I don't think the tree frog went very far. There seems to be a whole family of them residing on the unfinished back porch, as their lonely cry fills the night air.

The grandsons are intensely curious. Criss placed a hive of honeybees in the back yard and cautioned the youngsters to steer clear of them for awhile. "They are gentle bees," he explained, "but they are riled up because they have been moved. Later that day, Adrian came in the house crying bitterly. His feelings were hurt as well as his body. "I was just a'watchin' them," he sobbed as the tears flowed freely. "It just came out and bit me on the lip!" The bees have calmed down, but he gives them a wide berth.

They have all accumulated pets this spring, including rabbits, baby chickens and a kitten or two. Matthew incubated another duck which claims him as a mother and follows in his footsteps. Children need pets to learn responsibility for their well being, as well as for affection. There are sometimes deeper lessons to be learned. Many times it is a child's first confrontation with death, and although it is a hard thing to face, it is necessary. Jessica's pet rabbit met an untimely demise when it escaped from its box while they were gone and encountered an ugly bulldog. Late that night, the telephone rang while I was getting ready for bed. A tiny, heartbroken voice asked, "Mommaw, did you know Skipper got killed?" Gently, I said that indeed I did know, and was terribly sorry. Overcome by sobs, she wailed, "Mommaw, I can't stand it!" I was sympathetic, for I knew how she felt, but tried to explain that yes, she could stand it. "I know it hurts, Jessica, but we all lose things we love and we have to learn to let them go," I told her. "But I loved Skipper better than all the other rabbits," she protested. I still tried to comfort her. "He'll never be hungry or sick — and tomorrow you can have a funeral for him." "All right," she whispered.

The next day my mother was walking down the hill when she heard someone singing softly and melodiously. As she got closer, she spied two little girls with downcast countenances and sober behavior. "Was that you singing, Abigail?" she inquired. Her clear voice had brought the words plainly to Mom, "Oh, how sweet to rest in the arms of Jesus." "Yes," she admitted solemnly. "We are having Skipper's funeral." (Jessica's mother said it was a closed casket ceremony — they had kept the body too long!)

Later that week Abigail lost her pet rabbit also — same dog. Although she cried, she was a bit more philosophical. "We all have to go sometime, Mommaw," she told me. In the country, children are close to birth and death, and they learn some of the hard facts of life early. I still think it is the best place to raise our little ones, and blessed are the children who can roam the fields and woods, and grow up close to nature. Our youngest daughter, Crystal, who lives in Newark, Ohio, told me that she didn't want to have any babies until they could grow up as she did —

surrounded by cousins and country.
The Clay Herald
May 7, 1990

Dog days began with a steady, drizzling rain that slowly subsided as the day progressed. All week wisps of fog had clung to the mountain tops, a sure sign that the rain was not yet over. It brought to mind Mom's old adage, "Fog on the hills brings water to the mills." Another good way to distinguish a brief shower from an all-day downpour is to watch the chickens. A short shower will send the chickens scurrying to the chicken house for shelter, to emerge after it is all over. But if you see them stay out in the rain, scratching and foraging, you just as well get prepared for an all-day rain.

The recent rainy weather has been hard on my baby chickens. I have rescued one little fellow three times from a watery grave. Late one evening he got caught in a sudden downpour, and I found him on his back with his feet sticking straight up in the air. There was hardly a sign of life left in him, but a padded shoe box and a light bulb soon had him hale and hearty. The next time, the mother hen had upended a feed pan over him, and he was trapped for hours before I found him. He revived again, but the last time I thought he was a goner. I discovered he was missing from the rest of the flock, and found him mired down in a manure pile up at the barn. Miraculously, he recovered from that and is now as bright and perky as the rest. I have a feeling he could find his way to the shoe box and light bulb on his own.

Comet chickens must surely be the most gentle breed of chickens alive. My mother hen accepted day-old chicks with open wings, and her own "doodies" are about three weeks old. Even the older chickens welcomed the little newcomers to the family without an adverse peck.

However, one of our little chickens, a black banty, is an oddball. Randy's mother sent him to me because her own setting hens wouldn't have a thing to do with him, and made life quite unbearable for the tiny chick. Our setting hen took him just fine, but he simply did not want anything to do with the other chickens. We would put him in the coop, and he would beat us back to the house. He loved people. Talk about an identity crisis! I spent the day trying to get him to stay with the mother hen and little chickens, but as soon as I walked away he would follow me to the house with loud and frantic peeping.

Matthew and I went to check on him once and as we walked up the hill to the barn, we could hear his panic-stricken chirp. The other chickens were scratching contentedly around the barn, but he was stranded on the side of the hill. We found him perched on a fallen log, and as soon as he spied us, he hurried so fast that he fell off the log and tumbled end over end down the bank. Regaining his feet, he flew straight as an arrow to Matthew, who picked him up and cuddled him in his hand. His panicky cries changed to a contented peeping. "Aw, Mommy, that's pitiful," Matthew said to me.

I forgot to add that our tom turkey, Homer, has adopted the setting hen and her chicks. He struts around her pen all morning until I let her out, then follows her all day to protect her and her babies. We do have crazy, mixed up animals. Once I looked out and the tiny banty was following the turkey, while the other chicks were behind their mother.

I had to go to choir practice just as a summer thunderstorm was fast approaching. I told Criss to look out for the chickens. but I still worried about them when the storm hit in sudden fury. I need not have worried. Criss said when the first crack of thunder sounded, the baby banty was the first one to run in and creep under the mother hen. Maybe he thought, "any old port in a storm!"

The six-year-old grandsons, along with Jamie, their neighbor of the same age, have played Indian all week. Criss asked me why there were several piles of rocks and a cinder block in the front yard, and I asked him if he had ever tried to make a tepee out of a blanket and three sticks. My front porch looks like the city dump, but these things are valuable to the boys. There is a Pop Tart box with a long string attached to it, and on the other end is taped a wedge of wood. This is their walkie-talkie, and beside it are three sticks with twine tied on the end, and bent stick pins on the ends of the twine. An empty three-pound coffee can rests nearby; when Josh gets three more he plans to build a go-cart. I can't throw these things away.

Yesterday these three little Indians came into the house and asked me for a large grocery bag. They had homemade bows across their shoulders, and sticks for arrows were stuck down in a quiver. It seemed they needed the bag to collect some chicken and turkey feathers for a headdress. I heard Jamie tell Benji that Aaron said if only they had a rope they could lasso that old turkey Homer and get them some feathers. Suddenly it dawned on me why Aaron had a grass rope the day before trying hard to lasso my setting hen — until I caught him.

I figure that little banty better watch out.

The Clay Free Press, July 17, 1985.
The Charleston Gazette, July 19, 1985.
The Clay Herald, July 24, 1989

The telephone rang the other day and a pitiful, quivering voice asked, "Mommaw, can I come down?" It was Luke, my three-year-old grandson. Of course I told him to come on, and as I further inquired, I discovered that his daddy had spanked him (quite unjustly, Luke thought.) He continued his tale of woe in the same wavering voice, "I've packed my clothes — I'm leaving home for good!" He came down and spent the night, and we got along just fine except I made the mistake of leaving his grandpa's shampoo on the side of the tub while I gave him a bath. When I got him out to dress him, he looked up with beaming smile and said, "I made Poppaw a whole bunch of shampoo!" He had emptied the shampoo into the bathtub and filled the bottle with water. You would think that after raising six, I would know better.

It reminded me of the time when I was about six years old and got corrected for some misdeed, so I left home. I stuffed some of my clothes in a brown paper "poke" and headed for Eversons. I guess I was ashamed to tell Mrs. Everson that I was moving in with them, so I hid the bag of clothes behind the vines that grew on their porch. I played happily all evening, and at dusk I was relieved to see Larry coming after me. And that is the way it is — as night approaches, we begin to long for home.

The Clay Free Press
May 16, 1984

July shows the colors of deep summer as the bright blue heads of the chicory nod along the roadside. The pale, muted flowers of springtime have changed to the flamboyant oranges of the pleurisy weed and common day lily, and the woods are lush and green. The first hard, green berries appear on the elderberry, and the blackberries are turning red.

There are abundant wild foods now, such as the deep-fried locust bloom that Mike enjoyed last week at work. One of the men brought it already prepared, and heated it in the microwave oven. Mike said it was spiced with hot sauce in the batter, and was really tasty. It reminded me of the squash and pumpkin bloom that Daddy used to roll in flour and fry. Poke stalks are delicious when they are boiled for a few minutes, drained and rolled in cornmeal, and fried in hot fat. There are some treats that you find only in the hills.

The corn is beginning to tassel in the hot July sun, and the early apples are ripening and dropping from the trees. Wild sunflowers, black-eyed Susans, and Queen Anne's lace are blooming along the roadsides, adding a cheery note to the day. I read a magazine article that stated a certain county in New York was promoting an ordinance prohibiting weeds from growing there. Included in the list of weeds were Queen Anne's lace, or wild carrot, chicory, and other wild flowers. What would a landscape be without the delicate flowers of Queen Anne's lace? It is considered a delicacy by wild food enthusiasts, and we ate the "wild carrot" in our playhouses. I have a feeling that these plants will spring up wherever they want to — rules and regulations are not for wild things.

The Clay Free Press
July 11, 1984

July, with its sweltering days, severe storms and high humidity slowly steams its way out. It registered 103 last week on the front porch thermometer, and it felt as if you were breathing hot water. Saturday night another flash flood hit our little holler, a violent, raging storm of major proportions. The weather had been threatening all day, and by late evening ominous black clouds were piling up in the Belcher Hollow. The electricity went off suddenly, and the storm hit almost as abruptly. In fact, there was more than one storm that struck, and it seemed centered right over us. Criss had gone on to bed, and was sleeping "the sleep of the just," when I woke him up to see the creek. In all the years that we have lived here, I have never seen the creek come up so fast. We moved the car close to the front porch, and Criss began hastily dragging his water pump, dog box and sundry other items nearer the house. It was an eerie feeling to stand in the darkness and watch the water come up higher and higher. The creek from the Belcher Hollow soon became a river, and a willow tree fell at the culvert and blocked the road with its branches. Matthew's basketball came floating from the court across the road, hesitated for a minute on the bridge railing, then shot on down the creek. The muddy water began lapping around the rear tires of the car, and I began considering climbing the hill behind the house. Huge, unidentified objects bobbed on top of the water, and the bridge was soon covered, with logs and debris striking against it. A white, box-like building floated by — Sam's dog house. Fortunately, Matthew had the foresight to untie the big treeing Walker hound and fasten him to an outbuilding earlier in the day. The rain slackened and the water began almost immediately to recede.

We began to assess our damage, and surprisingly, the only casualty other than the dog house was my baby duck that was missing. We were fortunate — the storm had left in its wake devastation and ruin in other places. Many basements were flooded; washers, dryers and furnaces were filled with sand and mud. At the mouth of our holler, where Summer's Fork creek runs into Big Laurel, several mobile homes were washed off their foundations, and rolling, muddy water was up to their windows. Camping trailers were washed away, gardens were demolished, and shrubbery and lawns were ruined.

My baby duck was another story. We searched for him with a flashlight, but the raging flood waters had surely swept him away. He was such a brave little fellow. Granny Evie had given him to me just a few weeks before, as something had happened to all her ducks except this one. They died one by one on her farm pond, and she suspected they were swallowing honey bees. She prevailed on me to take this lone orphan and save him. I thought of how enthusiastically my white hen duck had taken to the half-grown female Mallard, and I replied, "Why sure — they'll love him." They didn't love him; they hated him. I didn't think of what I was doing to two spinster ducks who were enjoying a peaceful life together by turning loose a small, quacking stranger who tried to cuddle up to them. They nipped his neck and tiny wings until I rescued him and shut him in the chicken pen. Then he cried and complained until I turned him loose again to be greeted by the same cruel treatment. One night they nipped him unmercifully and I waded in the creek to catch him. It looked as if he shut his eyes and dove underwater like a yellow blur for ten or twelve feet. I scooped him up and put him in the pen again, where he crawled wearily to a corner and collapsed. After three or four days, however, I noticed them beginning to tolerate him, and the white duck actually began mothering him. The night the water washed him away, she swam back and forth across the roiling water, trying to find him.

I mourned a little, and the next morning, mixed

in with the birdsong, it seemed I could hear the peeping of a baby duck. I told Phyllis that I knew it was my imagination, but it seemed that one bird was singing like a duck. We were inspecting the water damage along the edge of the creek when Phyl suddenly yelled, "there's your duck!" Sure enough, that brave little duck was swimming gamely along the edge of the creek on the far side of the bank. I plunged in the waist-high water after him, and just as I reached him, he made another of those swift underwater dives and disappeared. Not a trace of him could we find. I went to the chicken lot and caught the white duck, falling on her in the process, and carried her down the bank where the little one had disappeared. I squeezed her a little to make her honk, and the baby duck began peeping furiously and magically reappeared. I set the motherly duck down; she immediately plunged into the water and led her adopted son out. Very proudly, she led him across the yard and back through the creek to the chicken pen. If ever a little duck deserves to live, he does. He is the pluckiest duck I have ever seen.

The Clay Free Press
July 25, 1984

A full moon, as round and shiny as a new penny, hangs suspended over our hills tonight. It bathes the hills and treetops in a golden glow, and creates dappled shadows in the hills and hollers. There is a hushed expectancy in the air, a feeling that something good is just about to happen.

It was nights such as this that we young people would band together and walk miles to attend a revival meeting. I sadly fear that it was not for any spiritual benefit, but it was a social event. Remember, about our only recreation was an occasional play party when we "gathered up" and played ring games, both young and old. We would walk to Grannies Creek or Valley Fork to church, and sit through the service pretending not to notice the young boys who crowded together on the back seat and eyed us. Usually their message was relayed through one of the smaller boys who sidled up to us after church and whispered, "Charley wants to know if he can walk you home." Welcome words — that was just what we came for. Then came the long walk home through the star-studded night — a lovely, magical evening scented with honeysuckle and sprinkled with youth. Today's teenagers would howl to the high heavens if they were asked to walk half a mile to do some errand, but we would walk six and eight miles in one night. (It never occurred to us that these same boys had to walk the return journey home late in the night after we were tucked safely in bed.)

We were a generation without automobiles, and used leg power to go everywhere. We were also a healthy bunch; you don't have a weight problem when you walk miles every week. It may not sound exciting to my grandchildren, but those moonlight strolls with the one you loved (or thought you did . . . the next week it might have been someone else) were high times in our lives.

My brother Mark was quite the gentleman when he was walking a girl home from church one night. They came to a huge mud puddle which stretched across the road. With a courtly gesture, he scooped the girl up in his arms and proceeded to carry her across. Unfortunately, the girl was heavier than he was and he dropped her right in the middle of the puddle.

You could say it put a damper on that romance.
The Clay Free Press
July 18, 1984

July slides smoothly into August and steamy late summer days. The jarfly sounds its queer, metallic drone above the hum of the bumblebee as he flits from flower to flower. In the soybean field, the wild morning glories run rampant, and the June bug flashes bright green, glistening wings in the hot sunshine. I caught one in the garden and was tempted for a little bit to tie a sewing thread on one of its legs and let it soar the way we used to when we were kids.

Like most country kids, we were fascinated by insects. Remember catching a Grandaddy Longlegs and chanting, "Grandaddy Longlegs, show us which way your cows have gone?" and then waiting until the insect put out one long, thin leg and pointed. In the dry, sandy soil under the Virginia office building, the doodlebugs built traps. Of course they were ant lions, but we never called them anything but doodlebugs. They made smooth funnels in the sand, like an inverted cone. We would creep close to the trap and croon, "Doodlebug, doodlebug!" until inevitably we would dislodge a grain of sand and we would see an upheaval in the surface of the funnel as the doodlebug came out to investigate. I don't ever remember catching one. And we would never kill a lady bug. We would catch them and throw them up in the air saying, "Lady bug, lady bug, fly away home. Your house is on fire and your children will burn."

We played with dry land turtles, or terrapins, which we called "torpins." They were hated by Mom, for they could ruin a tomato patch almost overnight.

We never killed them, but carried them up in the woods far away from the garden. I guess we figured the tomatoes would be gone by the time they came creeping back on their tiny bowed legs. We would pick the potato bugs off the vines and drop them in a jar of crude oil — perhaps not too humane, but better than poison insecticide. Mom wouldn't touch a worm, but it didn't bother me to pick off the vicious-looking tomato hornworm. We had to eliminate the pests somehow. I'll never forget the first summer our pastor put out a garden here. Fresh from the city of Baltimore, this was a foreign land and a strange culture. Mom caught him spraying his sweet corn one morning with Raid. "These pesky bees are all over the tops of my corn," he explained. He has never lived that down.

The Clay Free Press
August 1, 1984

The leaves hang limp and dispirited in the hot summer sun, knowing that their summer's work is almost finished. The underbrush along the roadbank is hot and dusty, giving no hint of the beauty yet to come. The air is full of the sound and smell of August. At night the crickets are beginning to play their melancholy tunes, and the doleful arguing of the crickets go on and on. "Katy did! She didn't! She did!" echoes through the night. Daddy used to say that it was six weeks until frost after the katydids started hollering. The tassels on the corn gives out a pleasant scent, and the almost too sweet scent of the milkweed bloom is carried on the breeze.

The Joe-Pye weed blooms above the purple blossoms of the horse mint, and the first yellow fronds of the goldenrod appear. In flower gardens, the regal

crimson heads of the August lily tower over the lowly
marigolds, and the showy hibiscus blooms in tropical
splendor. The birds still sing at daybreak, but their
lusty springtime song is honed down by a summer of
hard work.

Suspended between summer and fall, August is
a waiting month.

The Clay Free Press
August 8, 1984

Matthew just acquired a baby rabbit; a
purebred french Lop that looks and feels like a soft,
puffy marshmallow. I am determined not to get
attached to another animal, but this bunny likes me.
He looks as if his ears are on sideways, as they both
droop down on one side giving him a decidedly rakish
look. I keep saying "him" and we really don't know if
it is a "him" or a "her." My mother-in-law Peach and
her husband once took in a scrawny stray cat that
they dubbed "Old Ben." They treated him well, and
Old Ben got fat and sassy. One day they returned
home from a drive to find that Old Ben had presented
them with a fine litter of kittens. Dave sighed and
commented, "Well, I guess we'll just have to call him
"Ben Hur." We are calling this bunny Leonard, but we
may have to change it to Leona.

In a family our size, someone is always making
a blunder. Criss has been teased for years over the
sycamore tree that he cut down in the edge of the
yard. When it fell, it took my entire kitchen porch with
it. Our son-in-law Randy is walking in his footsteps.
He has spent weeks now fencing in his yard to make a
safe place for the baby to play. This week he sat back
and basked in the satisfaction of a job well done,
complete with metal posts and a new gate. To his

horror, he realized that he had completely fenced in a camping trailer. To make matters worse, it wasn't even his — it belongs to my sister.

The Clay Free Press
August 15, 1984

Many folks are feeling the pinch of the economy these days, and the ones who went through the depression could tell us a few things. Criss learned to "hobo" his socks when a hole was worn in the heel. When a mother was too busy chopping wood, hoeing corn, canning vegetables, milking, churning, cooking and raising a family to darn the offending hole, all you had to do was turn the sock around so that the hole was on top of your heel.

Back during the days when times were much harder, a large family lived up in the holler from us. One day they had unexpected company, and the mother sent one of the bigger boys to her mother's house for a chicken to cook. He dutifully went to Grandma's, collected his live chicken, and started home. As he went by our house, my brothers had a hot marble game in progress. He watched for a minute, then set his chicken down and joined the game. Of course the chicken headed home as fast as his chicken legs would carry him, and Dale finished his marble game and looked around for his chicken which was long gone. "Well, one chicken is good as another," he philosophized, as he headed for Mom's chicken lot and caught a fat hen. They had their chicken and dumplings, and Mom never missed the chicken. When she was told about it years later, she laughed.

The Clay Free Press
July 28, 1982

The days are growing a little shorter and in the summer melody there can be heard the first sad note of fall. I can hear a plaintive cheeping outside as the banty hen weans her last baby chicken. The little fellow frantically searches for his mother, and hasn't learned yet that he is a part of the flock. In a few days he will be scratching happily along with the rest of the chickens.

We had our family reunion here yesterday, and I thought of how we need this sense of belonging to a family. Even though we have left the parental nest, we need these times of getting together and strengthening the family ties. Wherever we roam, the family ties are still there, and the hills call us home.

While I was gone one day last week, one of my good neighbors asked to borrow some horseradish for a pickle recipe. Crystal was here, so she fixed it up and sent it to her — in an envelope. (This was prepared horseradish.) When she told me, I was scandalized. "Why didn't you send her the whole jar?" I asked. Well, she only wanted five teaspoonsful. Mom asked me if I had apologized to her and I told her, "Apologize? I can't even face her!" What do you say to a neighbor when you've sent her five teaspoons of cream-style horseradish — in an envelope?

The Clay Free Press
August 11, 1982

The sun slides behind the horizon this evening, leaving a deep pink afterglow. A flock of whippoorwills flicker briefly against the evening sky, then are gone. It seems all too soon for the birds to be gathering for their trip south, yet there is more than a hint of fall in the air. The mornings dawn cool and misty, until the midmorning sun burns off the mist and brings another fair day. The nights are cooler, and a blanket feels good before morning.

The purple ironweed has joined the goldenrod and Joe-Pye weed on the roadbank, and the land is taking on an autumn look. Sometimes when I get up early in the morning, and see the world freshly anointed with dew, the cobwebs shimmering with drops of crystal, I know why the Bible says, "And God saw everything that He had made, and behold, it was very good."

The cellar is beginning to fill up with bright jars of canned food, and brown-skinned potatoes fill the bin. Harvest time is a thankful time.

I am getting the urge to turn the house inside out and give it a good cleaning before cold weather. Housework takes second place to canning season, but the clutter and cobwebs are getting to me. Seems that every insect in the woods wants to move indoors; I found a katydid on the curtains yesterday. I have been sorting through some knick-knacks, trying to decide if I could discard some of them. There are so many memories connected with these things. I found salt and pepper shakers that the kids had brought back from Carnifax Ferry, the Great Smoky Mountains, and Grandfather Mountain in North Carolina. There were mementos from Grand Isle and Elmer's Island, Louisiana, that brought to mind the foaming waves that carried the marine life and sea shells to deposit them at our feet. Along with the memories of that trip, I packed them away.

I found the sea shell novelties that Patty had brought back from Myrtle Beach when she went with her friend Renee. She will want these. I picked up the spice rack that had belonged to Mrs. Everson, and was given to me by her daughter after she passed away. I loved her, and miss her still. I looked at the row of little yellow chickens and could see her kitchen again and almost hear her girlish giggle. I sighed, and tenderly put away the spice rack of chickens. Next was a decrepit pair of salt and pepper shakers that my brother Ronnie had given me when he was just a little shaver. He had sold garden seeds that spring, and for his premium had ordered Mom and me a set. Tarnished and battered, they would be cherished by no one except me. I rolled them up in a paper towel and returned them to the box. The only things left were a half-pint milk bottle from the Blossom Dairy that Criss had found years ago (which I had to keep) and a broken lamp. I did throw the lamp away.

I'll never be a good housekeeper. I can't throw away memories.

The Clay Free Press
August 29, 1984

August is gone; slipped away into that land called Yesterday. Summer is almost over, and the time of the singing birds and greening fields are nearly past. Another September has come; a gentle lady in a multicolored gown and a song in her heart.

On this cool, misty morning, Pilot Knob is shrouded in a blue veil, and the sun hasn't quite peeped through the white, riffled clouds that spread across the sky. The garden has the late summer fragrance of ripe corn tassels and milkweed blooms, and the fragile velvet of the wild morning glory is spread everywhere. It is a joy to be alive and able to enjoy the things God has made.

The vivid blue skies of September stretch from our hills to infinity, dotted here and there by a few white clouds. A playful breeze springs up, scattering a handful of premature brown leaves and sending them scudding across the ground. In the distance, the hills take on a yellow hue as the leaves begin their annual change to fall's spectacular colors. The stalk of the pokeberry turns a beautiful shade of purple and droops its purple-black fruit downward. As youngsters, we used to squeeze the berries to make lovely purple ink. I read where the early colonists used pokeberry juice for a dye, and also to improve cheap wine.

I wonder if Mom knew that when she used it for the same purpose one time. I guess most country boys try their hand at making homemade wine, and brother Ronnie was no exception. Mom was poking around our old barn one time, and happened to notice the edge of a jug sticking out from under some hay. Further investigation proved that Ronnie had sneaked out some of her canned blackberries and was trying his hand at winemaking. After sniffing the contents, Mom poured out the whole jug of contraband liquid, carefully filling the jug back up with water from the pond, and squeezed pokeberries in it to make an appealing wine-colored drink. Hiding the jug back under the hay, she went innocently about her business. My brother never mentioned the incident, but I would have loved to have seen his face when he sampled the finished product.

Grandpa O'Dell found a churn of home-brew that his boys were making, right in the middle of the fermenting stage. He took it to the hog pen, and poured it in the trough for the pigs. They guzzled it down and got roaring drunk. Grandpa would tell about it and slap his leg and laugh. "Them hogs went plumb wild," he would wheeze. "They run around the pen squealin' and staggerin' and then would fall down and waller!" Come to think of it, there's not too much

100

difference in hogs and men at times.

The Clay Free Press
September 5, 1984

The ground cherries are beginning to ripen between the dry corn stalks, and the elderberries are ready to make into jelly. (A slug of lemon juice is good in that.) I have never tried to make preserves from the ground cherries, but I love to eat the crunchy, yellow fruit out of hand. Our hills are rich in wild foods, and we need to take advantage of them.

My sister makes an absolutely delicious persimmon cake that rivals any fruit cake, and I have a recipe for a pawpaw pie. Pawpaws, that mountain version of a banana, makes a tasty snack. One little boy back in grade school will always be remembered by the pawpaws that he carried to school in his pocket. It reminds me of the lunch my father carried to Hagar school when he was a child — two baked sweet potatoes.

My grandson, Jeremy, came home from school after the first day and announced, "Guess what? — only 179 more days of school!" I loved school and would have gone on Saturday if possible. I can remember how excited we were the first day. Proudly decked out in our new dresses and stiff bibbed overalls, with new shoes that felt hot and strange on our feet after a summer of going barefoot, we marched to the foot of the steps and lined up to pledge allegiance to "Old Glory." Some children are not so glad, though.

As we come down to the second week of school, the little ones are becoming more or less adjusted to the bewildering process of the educational system. Our six-year-old grandson, Aaron, is having a hard time getting used to the first grade. He hates to get up early, so this morning his mother let him sleep in and drove him to school. They had an enjoyable time on the way there, and a good talk together. He jumped cheerfully out of the truck, kissed his mother good-bye, and skipped in the school. She came home quite relieved, but had been home only a few minutes when the school secretary called. It seemed that Aaron had been intercepted at the Valley Fork post office, hitchhiking his way home. The alert postmaster called the school, and the principal came and got him. Through his tears, Aaron informed the principal that he was sick and needed his mommy and daddy. Of course, his sickness was the familiar old malady known as homesickness, and he was promptly transported back to school. After being sternly reprimanded and warned about child molesters, we hope that he will keep his thumb in his pocket.

The Clay Free Press
September 7, 1983

I wish someone would tell me how to break up a setting hen. I have had three hens who persist in setting, although I throw them off the nest a dozen times a day. Mom told me she had read about putting them in cold water, as their body temperature raises when they are setting. This sounded logical to me, so I took them one at a time down to the creek where I plunged their fevered bodies in the cold water. When I finished the third hen, a little voice behind me spoke, "Mommaw, here's your cat," and handed me my baby kitten. I had forgotten about the little shadow that goes in and out with me — granddaughter Abigail who is two years old and generally one step behind me. I explained to her that we don't "do" the kitten, but something tells me that the cat is in for a baptismal service the first time my back is turned.

Flower gardens are at their peak this time of year. I was admiring a neighbor's this week, where the marigolds gleam like gold coins scattered on the green grass, and the Old Maids march primly in rows in their Sunday-go-to-meeting dresses. Scarlet sage glows crimson, and the touch-me-nots invite one to touch. I would love to have "yard flowers" as my husband calls them, but like my dream of someday being tall and slender, it is pretty improbable. It seems that my yard is forever destined to be embellished with dog houses and chicken pens; scraper blades and tractor wheels. Criss planted me a lovely wild honeysuckle bush three years ago. One day I saw two of my grandsons marching through the yard with branches draped across their shoulders. It was both halves of my honeysuckle bush. Well, someday my grandchildren will grow up. By then I will have great-grandchildren.

The Clay Free Press
September 14, 1983

True friendship is a treasure beyond price. Transcending time and distance, it stands ready to blossom and flourish again at a touch or a word. Last week I had the privilege of being with one of my oldest and dearest friends. The years fell away like dry leaves before a fall wind, and it seemed that the threads of our lives, once so closely interwoven, were waiting to continue a pattern of love. We laughed, and talked, and swallowed down a surreptitious tear, as we journeyed back through the poignant land of yesterday.

Ever since I can remember, I have known Myrtle

Belle. I was born in August; she in November of the same year. One of the earliest recollections I have of her was when we were about nine years old, and her mother had just passed away. She was a tiny girl, with innocent blue eyes and long dark braids. Mom had ordered me a sample bottle of Jergens hand lotion, and I was so proud of it. I felt sorry for her, and impulsively gave her my cherished bottle of hand lotion. As children often do, I instantly regretted my action. "When you use up all the lotion, I'd like to have the bottle back," I told her. I remember how kindly she offered the whole thing back to me. By then I was feeling very selfish. "No, you keep it," I told her. Myrtle Belle was always completely unselfish and giving of herself.

We grew, and the friendship grew. I spent much time at her house. After her mother died, leaving her father with ten children, they helped raise one another. They called their father "Early" and there was no tone of disrespect. Rather, it was like a title for a father and mother combined. I'm sure that many times we were a complete nuisance, yet Early never said a cross word to any of us. One boring Sunday afternoon, for lack of anything better to do, Myrtle Belle, Jeuell Beth and I jumped up and down on Early's foot bridge (made of two-inch pipe) until we bent it completely down in the creek. A little abashed, we slunk home, and the next day I tentatively asked Myrtle Belle what Early had said about the bridge. "He never said a word," she answered serenely.

Their home was a happy place, and I felt so welcome there. Other neighborhood kids must have felt the same, as overnight guests were the rule rather than the exception. Early loved children, and we knew it. His testimony in church always ended with an admonition to the young people. "Children, be good," he would say earnestly. And we wanted to, if just to please him. That is probably the secret as to how he raised ten children to be good parents, good citizens, and good neighbors. He expected them to be good.

And the memories kept coming. We laughed at how Glenville used to stay in bed until someone yelled that the school bus was in sight. I still can't figure out how he made it, unless he slept with his clothes on. We were recalling the socks that we made out of sweater sleeves when we were in high school, and Mary Ellen broke in with, "I thought I was the only one who wore those!" Shucks, Myrtle Belle and I invented them. They worked pretty well, except they had a tendency to bunch up on the top of your foot and make uncomfortable welts. I reckon we were poor, but we didn't know it, and thus we were not handicapped by the knowledge. Anyway, most of our friends were in the same boat. No, this was not the Great Depression — in fact, the year I started to high school, the motto of the graduating class was, "The forty-niners sought gold; we seek knowledge."

But time went on, and Myrtle Belle dropped out of high school to get married. I felt a loss, but soon I was married too, and we were having our babies. But there was a difference — Myrtle Belle had an ambition that I lacked. In the busy years of young motherhood, she managed to earn her high school diploma, then it was on to college. Then it was her Master's degree she earned. She taught school successfully for several years, now she is a school counselor for two of the elementary schools in Charleston. With her generous and compassionate spirit, I can think of no one more qualified to deal with troubled children.

And she has not changed. As secretary for the State Advisory Board of the Advent Christian Church, she does quite a bit of public speaking. "I just tell

them that I am one of ten kids from up a holler," she
says simply. "It breaks the ice, and someone can
always relate to that." Her eyes are still that innocent
blue; just a trifle weary now from shouldering too
many of her students' troubles. She loves her job as
counselor, but finds it hard to remain detached. I am
sure that many times she doesn't, and I'm confident
that the children love her.

Myrtle Belle Brown Arbogast — I'm proud to call
her my friend. She's one of Early's ten kids from up
this holler — and one in a million.

The Clay Free Press
March 16, 1983

A SEASON OF GOLD

Summer is dying. You can hear it in the funereal chant of the crickets singing their sad song night and day. You can see it in the dry, dead leaves as they fall, crisp and brown, into the dry creek bed. You can feel it in the increasing coolness of the nights; in the chill of the early morning. You can smell it in the dying vegetation of the garden, the dry rustle of the cornstalk, and in the warm, nutty fragrance that rises from the earth itself as the sun bathes it in hot rays. You can sense it as the days grow shorter, night falls earlier, and dark lingers longer each morning. The birds sense it as they grow restless and gather up their flocks to move to a warmer climate where summer lives and thrives.

There are signs of the demise of summer all about us. Cords of firewood, neatly cut and stacked, line sheds and porches. The cellar bulges with its rows of canned goods, and the barns are filled with hay for wintering the livestock. The apple trees groan and creak under their burden of red and gold fruit. We are holing up some for the winter; in lieu of a root cellar, we have an old deep freezer buried in the ground. Potatoes, cabbage and turnips are all good stored this way.

Chipmunks and squirrels scramble madly to gather nuts and grain for the winter ahead; they too know that summer is dying. The striped chipmunks have worn a path to our corncrib as they prepare for winter weather. I wonder if they get the same secure feeling that we do when they know they are prepared.

Shiny chestnuts slip out of their burrs and drop silently on the still-green grass beneath the tree. The shell-bark hickory nuts are falling among the yellow leaves; tempting squirrel and hunter alike to gather all they can carry. Black walnuts await the softening effect of rain and frost to tender their hulls so they can be harvested. Late apples ripen and fall, and pawpaws slowly turn soft and delicious. The Lord has blessed us with so much beauty and bountiful goodness from the earth.

The Clay Free Press
September 26, 1984

The rainy, wet weather of last week has been replaced by cool, dry air and blue skies. Fat white clouds float by leisurely, to drift apart and re-form in marshmallow manner. Orange touch-me-nots border the creek banks and the goldenrod is spread everywhere in yellow masses. A full moon hung in the sky last night, while the sleepy chirping of the katydids and crickets lulled us to sleep. September is a joy to the soul.

As the kids have settled down in school, my mind went back to my own grade school days. In memory I walk the road to Hagar, climbing the hill to the school. There were butterflies of excitement and apprehension in my stomach, and I could smell again the trash barrel burning — that unique and not unpleasant odor of pencil stubs, bits of crayon, and paper. On past the wellhouse, we stand lined up before the tall steps, saluting the flag as she waved proudly from her tall flagpole. We marched up the steps into our respective classrooms; to the "little" room for the primary grades, and the "big" room for the lordly upper grades. I smelled again the chalky smell of the blackboard, and could see the letters of the alphabet hanging on the wall of the little room — big and little letters. My arm ached as I remembered the Palmer method of handwriting, and the swooping O's and M's we made with our whole arms. I could hear Miss Carper again saying, "Now, children," and read again from our "Peter and Peggy" first grade book.

"Peter is a boy. Peggy is a girl. Peter has a dog. Peggy has a cat. Peter's dog is big and brown. Peggy's cat is little and white." I worked arithmetic problems on the board, and read again about the circus monkey that fell into a barrel of tar. What an honor it was to be picked to dust out the erasers at the end of the day! I skipped down the hill to the girl's toilet — and remembered how may trips were made while "books were taken up" just for a break in routine. I heard Mr. Hinkle ring the bell to summons us back into the schoolhouse after recess was over. Hot and tired from the games of tag, draw and prisoner base, we trooped back to our classrooms.

We had no fancy playground equipment, or blacktopped lot, yet I am sure that no one had more fun playing than we did. The boys played endless games of marble; the girls jumped rope incessantly. We had a heavy rope that would whack a hefty welt on the skinny shinbone of a little girl who missed a jump. We would chant, "Johnny crossed the ocean, Johnny crossed the sea, Johnny broke the milk bottle, and laid it on to me. I told Ma, and Ma told Pa, and poor old Johnny got H-O-T." When we got to that point, we would turn the rope as fast as we could. It took a good jumper to keep up with that.

We played longtown mostly at the noon hour, which was a form of softball. It seemed the hour was too short to play all the things we wanted to play. We would hear the old hand bell ringing out its summons, and the cry, "Books are taking up" would go from child to child.

Day's end would find us trudging home, carrying our shoes and the lesson we had done that day. The smell of supper cooking would drift out to meet our noses, and the younger children would rush to meet us as long-lost travelers.

The two-room schoolhouses are relics of the past, and perhaps they have outlived their usefulness. I am thankful for the memories I have of my first eight years of schooling, and I wouldn't trade them for the most modern means of education devised.

Hagar School is gone now, the big beech trees that supplied us with the biggest and tastiest beechnuts I have ever seen are gone, and so are many of the teachers and some of the students — but memories linger on.

The Clay Free Press
September 8, 1982

The air has a decided nip to it this morning, but the sun sends down fingers of light that warm the waking earth. The goldenrod sends out its own warm sunshine, and the bright-eyed asters bask in their glow. Early morning is my favorite time of the day. There is a hushed expectancy that hovers over the earth, as nature seems to pause before the serious business of the day begins. Last night's fervent symphony by a multitude of night insects has dwindled to a muted hum, and a solitary songbird lifts a voice of praise unto its Creator. I need this time of quietness to commune also with my Creator. Before the rush of the day begins, and the world presses hard upon me, this time is necessary. No wonder that the Lord God liked to walk with man in the cool of the day. As I wander about the yard, I pause to admire the perfection of a full-blown rose; each perfect petal glistening with dew. Only God could create the intricate beauty of a rose. I see His handiwork in all nature about me; in the majesty of the hills and in the glory of the sunrise. My heart sings in praise to our Father and the Maker of this world. The strength and grace that I receive through this quiet time of prayer and meditation is a warm glow that stays with me throughout the day.

September is a good time to wrap up the tag ends of the garden; to make soup mix or tomato soup, or pickle the last nubbins of corn. I always enjoy meandering through the garden for the last mess of scrappy half-runner beans — Daddy always said it was the best one of all. We put out a couple of rows of Logan Giant beans in the field corn this year and hope to harvest enough for a few messes.

It seems only a breath ago that the fragrant apple blossoms, pink and white, hung on the apple trees. Now the ripe apples, red and juicy, are falling on the ground, ready to be harvested. Time does fly by on pale, whispery wings, to brush your cheek for just an instant and then is forever gone. It was just a short time ago that my brothers and sisters and I were in school, then it was my own children, and now it is my grand-children. The days speed by. There never seems to be enough time in the day to do all the things that need to be done. The seasons seem to come closer and closer together; even the years flow one into another with incredible swiftness. I want to enjoy all my days here, and be ready to leave when God calls me home.

Our pastor's daughter was spending the night with Crystal last week, and while looking through an old photo album, she found a snapshot of Crystal and her when they were about five years old, complete with snaggle-tooth grins and knobby knees. "Oh, those were the good old days," she sighed wistfully. (Shelly is thirteen.) Criss got tickled and asked her if she knew when the good old days were. "They're right now," he told her. He was right as usual. Too many times we miss out on enjoying the "now" because we are looking back in the past, or forward into the future. "Now" is all we really have. We had better make the most of it.

The Clay Free Press
September 14, 1983

Waiting autumn waits no longer, but hums her own sad-sweet song as summer departs. It is a mournful litany sung by a thousand cricket voices, bemoaning summer's end. It is a melody composed of crisp, frosty mornings, and the smell of wood smoke hanging in the air. The air is crisp as a Winesap apple, with a mellowing up in the day when sunshine warms the earth again. I enjoy being a housewife during autumn more than any other time. With the garden all gathered in, and the fruits of our labors stored in the cellar and freezer, there is time now to bake and sew; to dream and rest. With the first snappy, cooler days, my mind goes to baked apple dumplings and homemade cookies. Keeping the cookie jar full for a bevy of grandkids is a monumental task.

Two of my little grandsons and I went up to the pond today to feed the ducks; two snow-white hen ducks and two proud Mallard ducks. The ducks sailed gracefully on the surface of the pond, stopping only long enough to dart their heads underwater for the bread we threw to them. The sun shone warm on our backs, counteracting the slight chill that seemed to emanate from the shady nooks and the water's surface. Clumps of wild asters crouched in pale blue mounds around the edge of the pond, and the tall goldenrod swayed above the boys' heads. It was such an appealing place that we were reluctant to come home. In two or three weeks the leaves will have turned in earnest, and the beauty will be such that our souls seem too small to contain it all. Even now, the greenbrier trails its chain of scarlet leaves up the roadbank, and on the dogwood tree the tiny red berries glisten. It is a joy to be alive, and living in the hills of West Virginia in the fall.

October came in on cloudy, gray feet and touched our hills with warm, damp fingers. Above the clouds, the blue skies of October wait impatiently to caress our ever-changing landscape. The hills are dotted with the brilliant reds of the sourwoods and maples, and the yellow gleam of the poplars and hickories. There is never a month in the year when the sky is such a blazing shade of blue. It is a fruitful month with ripe pawpaws and persimmons; hazelnuts and chestnuts. The lightest breeze brings down a shower of golden beech leaves, and there is a metallic tinkle as the ripe beechnuts fall on the tin roof of the corn crib. It is a day to soothe the soul.

The sun went down this evening with red skies and promises of a fair day tomorrow. A thin sickle moon cuts sharply through the sky, and the night is hushed and still. Tied to his dog house, our 'coon dog, Sam, grows restless, as if he feels the pull of the moon and senses that 'coon season is almost here. It almost makes me want to go 'coon hunting.

Enjoy these beautiful days, for the cold hand of winter will soon be upon us. Take a hike, pick up some walnuts, gather some hazelnuts, absorb a sunset. Thank God for the beauty that He has made.

The Clay Free Press
September 28, 1983

One gloomy day last week my oldest son Mike telephoned and asked me to go with him to hunt some mushrooms. The meadow mushrooms that pop up during warm, wet, fall weather abound in his fields, and he was taking my mother. At first I hesitated; it was early morning and still chilly, and I was getting ready to clean the back porch. "Fall is wasting," he reminded me, so I grabbed a sweater and an old pair of shoes, and we headed for the pasture fields. As soon as we reached the top of the hill, the sun broke through the clouds. It shone on the tender white mushrooms, with the pink petticoats, that were flung over the meadow. The ground had the sweet, dry smell of fall, and the crickets chirped their good-bye to summer. A chipmunk protested noisily at the intruders on his home ground, but we ignored him and gathered a panful of mushrooms. We searched a pawpaw grove in vain for ripe pawpaws, but found a tree full of hard, yellow apples. The sunshine glinted on the farm pond, dry leaves floated gently to the ground, and the pastoral scene breathed peace and contentment. We were three generations enjoying the fall day together.

Loading us into his four-wheel drive vehicle, Mike headed up a narrow, steep road that was more suitable for a goat than a car. Winding around steep curves, across deep ruts, and straight up the hillside, he climbed until the road ended. From the top of that hill, there was a heart-stopping view. We could see row upon row of undulating hills garbed in their fall colors. In the distance, they resembled a vast patchwork quilt worked in harmonizing shades of brown, scarlet, orange and yellow. Bright green squares of meadow land contrasted with the groves of yellow poplar, beech, and white ash. Maples glowed crimson, as did the scarlet oak and dogwood, and nothing outshone the sumac clad in its cloak of red. The faraway ridges faded to a smoky blue, and on the

very top of the hill where we stood, showy goldenrod
bloomed beside clumps of wild blue asters, and the
grove of sassafras waved hands of orange and yellow.
It was a day to long remember.

The Clay Free Press
October 17, 1984

A brisk fall wind sends dark clouds drifting
across a leaden sky, and bends the tall goldenrod to
and fro in a graceful, dipping dance. It picks up the
smoke from the chimney and wafts it heavenward, and
sets the wind chimes on the porch all a'jingle. The
wood fire feels good on this chilly day, and a pot of
brown beans bubbles on the stove and sends forth a
homey smell. The wild asters are blooming right up to
the kitchen door; their blue-fringed eyes watching us
come and go.

I have been reading a wild food cookbook, and
it gives me a strong urge to go out and dig up some
roots and cook them — or at least cook some wild
artichokes or stew a few day lily buds. I guess the idea
of living off the land appeals to the pioneer in most of
us.

Last Sunday afternoon the kids and I took a
long walk through Ash Camp just after we had
polished off a big fried chicken dinner with all the
trimmings. We pretended that we were lost in the
wilderness with no food and had to live off the land.
We got into the spirit of the game so much that we
really felt famished, and a couple of the kids almost
got into a fight over one deerberry that they found. We
do have an abundance of wild foods here in the hills,
and we utilize quite a few of them. I love poke greens
in the spring, and fall brings pawpaws and
persimmons, as well as a variety of nuts. Many

families depend upon wild game for their table, and some housewives welcome the crop of wild grapes for their jams and preserves.

I'll never forget the first persimmon that Patty ate. She came in the house with a strange, twisted look on her face and told me, "Mommy, I picked this little green apple and ate it, and all at once I couldn't breathe!" Just like the wild grape, the persimmon must be touched by frost to be good.

Squirrel season will soon be upon us, and it is time to finish the last minute chores and wrap up the tag ends of summer. Piles of wood, stacked and dry, attest to the fact that many people have been as diligent as the ant and not fiddled their summer away like the grasshopper. Criss and the boys have downed several trees and have our firewood all cut and stacked for the winter. He has come a long way since he felled the sycamore tree that took my back porch with it.

The tender young leaves of the mustard and kale greens are ready to pick, and the turnips have formed fat bottoms. I think I will pick a nice mess of greens and let the wild asparagus grow for another week.

The Clay Free Press
September 29, 1982

The day dawns clear and cold, and at six-thirty it is still dark. The stars are shining, a little dimmer now since thin fingers of light over Pilot Knob herald the rising of the sun. The light spreads, turns rosy, and the sun rises on another fair day. As Matthew says, "It feels like a squirrel huntin' day."

The men and boys in our family have been getting their share of the bushy-tailed, little creatures, as they are plentiful this year. I could never kill one;

sometimes it gives me a pang to see the boys bring one in with a nut still clamped in its jaws. But when they are cooked nice and tender, and served with squirrel gravy and sweet potatoes, that is a different story.

My sister Jeannie's family have an old beagle named Buster who has just about retired from active rabbit duty. His eyesight and hearing are poor, and he'd rather lie in the yard and sleep than anything else. The family was sitting on the porch the other day when a rabbit hopped through the yard. Old Buster slept on, dreaming no doubt of rabbit chases and young, agile legs. Eric called him; he raised his head and dropped back to sleep. Eric ran over, picked him up, and began chasing the rabbit with Buster in his arms. At the top of the bank he dropped the bewildered dog, who tumbled back down the hill still wondering what the fracas was all about. He never did see the rabbit.

Buster is all heart, though. Betty, a young female beagle who was expecting puppies, joined the family, and he befriended her right away. She was full of vim and vigor, and every morning would roust Buster from his pleasant slumber for merry rabbit chases and happy gambols through the woods. This went on until her puppies were due, then she disappeared. They searched for her without success. A few days later Julie spied Buster crossing the road with a piece of bread in his mouth. They investigated further, and found Betty curled up under an oil rig, with one little puppy by her side. She was snug in her maternity ward while faithful Buster carried her meals to her. It may be a May-December match, but the little family seems quite content. The new puppy, little Dixie-Flyer, is thriving and Buster is one proud father.

Criss used to be a fervent coon hunter until time and age took its toll. I went with him a few times.

The first time I went, we were in Jackson County, and I set out full of energy and high hopes. I had on a pair of his five-buckle arctics (size 12) over my shoes, and every step I took, I had to take three inside the boot. By the time we had gone a mile, I had walked three. I was terrified of copperheads out there and cautiously watched every step I took. We would rush pell-mell straight up the mountain, through brier thickets, over fallen logs, and under barbed wire fences. Every time Criss stopped to listen for the dog, I would look warily around for snakes. I finally got so exhausted that I would fling myself down on the ground to rest, snakes or no snakes. I figured they'd have to look out for themselves.

We didn't have much luck that night, but the next morning at daybreak, we heard Old Smoky barking treed. We got out of bed and went to him, and he had a yellow coon treed up a big poplar. It was the first one I had ever seen. I decided then that coon hunting wasn't quite my calling.

The Clay Free Press
October 27, 1982

This cooler weather sharpens appetites, and we always begin the day with a hearty breakfast. Country breakfasts are bountiful, and my family can't imagine breakfast without hot biscuits. Mom always fixed a big breakfast; in addition to the bacon or ham and eggs, we had to have something to sop our biscuits in. Sometimes it would be creamed tomatoes or hot jam made with canned blackberries, or cooked apples. I used to love to stay all night with Peggy Ann Hanshaw. We slept upstairs many nights in the big, two-story house; our bed heaped with a half-dozen homemade quilts. Her mother made "chocolate syrup" or "chocolate gravy" as some called it, and hot biscuits. We loved it. I remember one time when the biscuits didn't turn out as well as usual, and her mother was fretting about them. "I don't know what is wrong with the biscuits this morning," she fussed. "They didn't raise at all." Reva Jarvis was spending the night that time, too. She looked up sweetly and said, "They tried, Aunt Beulah — they squatted!"

Mom's family ate a lot of the chocolate gravy, too — only they called it "co-ca." It was made with milk, and eaten with a lump of butter in it. Some of these things are almost a thing of the past. My mother-in-law ate "soakies" which was a hot, buttered biscuit crust that she covered with hot coffee laced with plenty of cream. Her family ate "poor-do," which we called "poor man's gravy" — simply brown gravy made with flour, bacon grease and milk. It is fancied up now with sausage and sold in fast food restaurants.

When we were all at home, there were eleven of us seated around the big dining room table for each meal. Many things, especially desserts, had to be doled out in shares. My brother Mark always saved his treat until the rest of us had eaten ours, and then right in front of us, with much feeling, he would eat his dessert slowly and tauntingly. I recall one hot summer Sunday when Mom served homemade butterscotch pie. As usual, the rest of us gulped ours right down, but Mark saved his. We were out on the back porch when Mark brought his piece of pie out with a smirk and much smacking of his lips. Unbeknownst to little brother, however, a yellow jacket had lit on his fork. Watching us, he popped it in his mouth with the next bite. It stung him on the tongue, which hung out of his mouth the rest of the day. Sad to say, some of the onlookers thought it was fitting justice. It has been a cardinal rule in our family ever since the children were small, that if you didn't have enough to share, you didn't eat it in front of anyone else. I guess that is a throwback to my childhood.

Kevin used to stand on Opal's store porch and wait until someone made a purchase. When they opened a candy bar or a soft drink, he would run home to say breathlessly, "They're eating stuff in front of me!"

The Clay Free Press
October 4, 1983

The moon rides high in the sky, a silver orb that shines coldly, a few black, wispy clouds floating over its surface. The wind blows in gusts, picking up the dry leaves in its path to toss in a mad, swirling dance. It is a night when anything can happen.

We hillbillies have always been a superstitious bunch. When I was a kid, tokens were my secret terror. You never hear much about them anymore, and I asked my mother why. She laughed and said it was because there wasn't any such thing, but when I was little they were discussed as an accepted fact. Tokens were an omen or warning of someone's impending death. Families and friends, gathered around the fireplace, would sit late in the night discussing the strange things they had seen and heard.

There was that light they had seen when Granny Cottrell had died. Neighbors had gathered at her home to keep vigil as it seemed she had only a little longer to live. Some of the young men were grouped in the kitchen to keep a fire in the old cookstove, when one of them glanced out the window. There was a light, like the beam of a flashlight, shining on the chicken house. He wondered aloud at the reason for it, and a couple of the other boys joined him at the window. While they watched, the spot of light grew larger until it was a huge circle covering the side of the building. It gradually grew smaller and smaller, until it diminished into a pinpoint and vanished completely. At that precise moment, two women who had been at the bedside of Granny Cottrell stepped in the room to announce that she had passed away just then.

When Grandpa Huge lay on his deathbed, a strange dog came and sat outside our window for two nights in a row and howled at two o'clock in the morning. The third night, Grandpa Huge died at two o'clock. The night before Grandpa O'Dell died, the rocking chair in the living room began to rock for no earthly reason.

There were dreams and premonitions that could never be fully explained. My mother possessed what we call ESP, and she lightly passed it off as being the seventh daughter. One night we were out in the yard, looking up at an eerie moon, all spotted and dark-streaked. "There's blood on the moon tonight," I remember hearing her say. "When there's blood on the moon, death lurks in the shadows." That very night, one of our neighbor's boys, whose nickname was "Moon" fell off the back of a truck and was killed. For awhile, I was almost afraid of my own mother. I got so afraid of seeing a token that I wouldn't go to the barn in broad daylight to get the dry onions we stored there.

It was in this kind of atmosphere that Uncle Grover walked home one dark night many years ago. There was no road to their home down on Big Laurel, just a path out the ridge, around a graveyard, and down over the hill. Uncle Grover was very near-sighted, the night was dark, and he was alone. Just as he neared the cemetery fence, he caught the glimpse of a ghostly white shape moving slowly through the cemetery. He stopped in terror, the blood draining from his body. While he watched, it shimmered and moved closer to him. Sheer horror lent wings to his feet and he started to run in blind panic. As he plunged headlong through the brush and weeds, he fell suddenly over a huge black shape that was warm and alive. As it lumbered to its feet with a startled "Moo," he realized it was the neighbors cows that were peacefully chewing their cuds along the graveyard fence. The trip on home was made in record time.

I hope I never see a token.

The Clay Free Press
October 28, 1981
The Charleston Gazette
November 1, 1991
The Clay Herald
October 28, 1991

The leaves are falling on Stony Lonesome. They are drifting down on Pilot Knob; covering the ground at Ash Camp. The big beeches are turning loose their little golden-brown ones, while the maples blow red, yellow and orange; twisting and turning in the breeze. The tall gum stands with its edges trimmed in scarlet.

The pranking season of Halloween looms very close, and this holler has had its share of hanky-panky. Ever since I can remember, it has been a tradition to block the road and throw water on the unsuspecting motorist who gets out of his car to remove the roadblock. There is a rock cliff above the road for the pranksters to store their water, do their dirty work, and then make a getaway into the woods. This practice, of course, is frowned upon by the older generation, and we were strictly prohibited from taking part in it. I can truthfully say that I never did, but I can't truthfully say that some of the others didn't.

One Halloween Daddy was working at Bayard, West Virginia, and Mom was staying there with him. Susie had joined the Rock Cliff Crowd, and as traffic was light that night, they got tired and wanted to go home. Susie insisted that they stay until Daddy came through, and about midnight she drenched her own father. She ran through the woods like a deer, beat them home, and jumped in bed with all her clothes on. She was sweetly in slumber when Mom and Daddy arrived, and she could hear Mom storming, "We came all the way from Maryland", she preached, "And didn't have a lick of trouble until we got in sight of the house!" Susie slept on. It was over a year later that she confessed to them that she was the culprit.

The Rock Cliff Crowd hasn't always gotten off scot-free. One year as they ran through the woods to get away, Jim Summers had stored his dentures in his shirt pocket. As he ran, they bounced out and Ronnie crunched them underfoot as he was running along behind him. Our Patty paid a little more.

She dressed to go out and "trick or treat," and as she left, we firmly forbade her to have any part in the water throwing. Unknown to us, she and some of the other teenagers had made plans earlier in the day to do their dirty work. They were having a ball upon the rock cliff, throwing water and running, when one of our neighbors stopped his pickup truck to remove the roadblock. He isn't exactly hirsute, and Patty yelled irreverently, "Watch out, Baldy!" as she came down on him with a bucket of water. No sooner did the water hit than he began whizzing rocks at them. "Man, I didn't know he could throw rocks like that!" Patty said later. "They were coming at us like bullets!"

They ran through the brush in a panic, and in the melee, Patty ran a stick in her eye. It was a severe injury that put her to bed for most of the week, during which period she had to listen to me preach about the wages of sin and reaping what you sow. It still flares up once in awhile, so she is still paying. I made her go apologize to our neighbor, and these are her own words, "Mom made me come apologize, but I am not sorry!" He laughed.

One of the funniest incidents happened several years ago, when Ronnie and some of the current boys were whooping it up at Halloween down at the bus house (where they blocked the road.) They had built up a fire and were waiting for a car to come through so they could throw water. While they were waiting, someone threw a shotgun shell in the fire which exploded and struck Rodney Braley in the leg, inflicting quite an injury. Just then a car pulled up, and all the boys ran except Rod, who managed to crawl in the bus house. They threw water on the man as he was moving the log, and out of the car jumped his wife, who was fighting mad. She was a tiny old woman who wouldn't have weighed more than ninety pounds soaking wet, but she was full of sound and fury. She waded in on poor Rod, who cowered in the bus house, wounded and bleeding. The other boys were on the hillside, rolling and laughing, as she beat him with an umbrella. Finally Dink White had mercy on him and quit laughing long enough to rescue him and drag him out by the shirt collar.

I've noticed that it was generally the women who got mad — the men usually took it in good heart. Perhaps they were remembering their own boyhood pranks. One Wednesday night a couple were on their way home from church when they found the road blocked. The man got out to move the roadblock, and was promptly soaked. It made his wife furious, so she jumped out of the car shouting, "Let's see you throw it on a woman". They did.

I don't go out on Halloween night.

The Clay Free Press
October 13, 1982

We had a power failure yesterday afternoon that lasted until after dark last night, and we got a taste of yesteryear as we prepared supper and got ready for church. As I mashed potatoes the old fashioned way by candlelight and the glow of an oil lamp, I thought of how we take these modern day blessings for granted. No power means no water in our area, so also with no shower we dressed and went to church. It was a precious service by the light of the flickering candles and oil lamps that cast shadows on the wall and gave out the homey smell of warm kerosene. A couple of Coleman lanterns shone in bright contrast, and I thought of how relative light is. When we moved back from Davis Creek, where we had used oil lamps, I can remember how glaring the gas lights seemed. (I'm sure many of you remember the gas lights — and those fragile mantles that a rambunctious kid would knock off by jumping around too much. And Mom's cry of anguish, "Oh, that was my last mantle!") When we had our house wired for electricity, it was a seven day wonder. We wandered from room to room flipping on the lights for the pure pleasure of seeing light. And that radio! It stood taller than the smaller children, and opened a whole new world to us. I remember "Terry and the Pirates," "Henry Aldrich," and "Dagwood and Blondie." "The Grand Ol' Opery" was not to be missed. Most Saturday nights, Daddy and I would stay up and listen until Minnie Pearl and Rod

Brassfield said their last "good-night." Radio was clean and decent then, and I wish it were so now.

Even a little candle will give light in a dark place, especially when there is no other light around. That is when it is needed most. Let us shine!

A soft, enveloping rain has ended our week of beautiful Indian summer weather. The mild mornings that smelled like hickory nuts are gone, so is the blue haze that outlined our hills and melted into the glorious sunsets at evening. The last sunny day brought a strong tang of woodsmoke, and I wondered if the particular smoky haze that characterizes Indian summer was caused by prairie fires that were rampant during that time.

I remember the woods fire that our two oldest children got out one fall when they were small. They had been playing in the woods back of the house that day when one of them ran in all out of breath to tell me that the woods were on fire. Fortunately, there were neighbors near who rushed to our aid, and the fire was quickly extinguished. It was a scary experience, even though the area burned was quite small. After the excitement had died down, I began gathering up the tools they had taken to fight the fire. I found, in addition to the hoes and rakes, a post hole digger, a spud, and two sledge hammers. They fixed the blame on one of the little neighborhood boys, whom they accused of playing with matches, and he was swiftly punished. While I was scouring the woods for the remnants of our tool shed, I came upon a curious sight. A soup can of water was bubbling merrily on the top of a still smoldering stump. Now as suspicious as well as puzzled, I decided I'd better question the kids further. When we got down to the bottom of it, as Daddy used to say, they confessed that they had built the fire on the stump to cook their "play dinner." They got a double dose of "birch tea" — one for playing with fire and the other for bearing false witness.

How I remember that birch tea — or it could be peach tree tea, or even apple — just whatever was the handiest. Mom whipped the most frequently, but Daddy whipped the hardest. It didn't take too many from him to do us. The worst tea of all was made with the keen willow switches. They were long and supple, and made us dance a jig. One of the worst punishments of all was to have to go get our own switches. If we brought back a weed, or something else unsuitable, Mom would go get her own and then we would really get it. I know it is not fashionable to paddle children now, but all seven of us children have grown into respectable adults and none of us has ever been in serious trouble. I can't help thinking that we would have less rebellion and delinquency among our youth today if the proper "teas" had been applied to the appropriate spots of their anatomy.

The Clay Free Press
November 10, 1982

Purple shadows linger on Pilot Knob, where the once-bright leaves have fallen from the trees. The red oaks are the last to shed their mahogany dresses, and they make a brilliant contrast against the green of the pines.

They make a satisfying crunch underfoot, and are a delight for the children to romp in and play. We used to rake up a huge pile of the dry leaves and play "Poor Robin." Remember the old song, "Poor Robin is dead, and layin' in his grave; Boo hoo hoo!" The subsequent verses went, "There grew a tall apple tree over his head" "The apples got ripe and ready to fall"

"There came an old woman a'pickin' them up" "Poor Robin jumped up and started to run" — it was terrifying when "Robin" jumped up out of his leafy grave and began chasing us. If there is anything that makes you want to be a kid again, it is the crisp, crunchy leaves of fall.

Deer season is upon us, and the hunters in our family are making preparations to go on that hunting trip. I do hope my son-in-law gets his deer this year. His last few trips have netted him several deer tracks and a couple of snorts. Patty says those deer snorts make mighty thin soup. I do like good venison that has been properly field dressed, then cut up right and cooked with a sprinkle of garlic. Food tastes so good this time of year when the appetite is sharpened by fall's chilly air. The time is right for a big pot of vegetable soup, turnips, kale and mustard greens, and pones of crusty corn bread. It's time to knock the frost off the pumpkin and transform it into some spicy pumpkin pies. I saw a recipe for pumpkin soup the other day, but I don't think I want any. Mom used to singsong an old phase she'd heard back in her childhood, "Corn bread and punkin butter's all we got to eat." Now that is hard up.

This cold weather makes me think of butchering time again. We used to kill our hogs at Thanksgiving, and I dreaded it. Daddy would heat washtubs of water to the boiling point, then go to the hog pen with his gun. We would cover our ears so we couldn't hear the crack of the gun or the poor things squealing. I liked to watch them scrape the hair from the carcass, after covering the animal with coffee sacks until the steam softened the bristles. The skin would emerge pink and clean, then the carcass would be hoisted high on a pig pole with a single tree through the tendons in the back legs. As soon as the entrails were removed, Daddy would put the heart and liver in a dishpan and take it to Mom. Our first mess of pork was usually liver fried with onions. Ribs and backbones would be cooked together for the next meal. Mom would grind fresh horseradish that grew in our back yard, mix it with vinegar, and serve it with fresh pork. It was delicious.

The real mess came later, when we had to grind the sausage on an old hand grinder. This was powered by muscle, and a lot of it was kid muscle. I hated the smell of lard rendering, and it seemed that grease was plastered on everything in the kitchen. But the end result was worth all the hard work.

Daddy cured the hams and bacon, then smoked them in the smoke house. We would hang them in the rafters there and slice off pink, sugar-cured slices of ham until up in the summer. That fried ham swimming in its own gravy was the best food in the world.

I guess there's nothing like a child's appetite, whetted by cold air and hard work, to make food taste good.

The Clay Free Press
November 9, 1983

I wonder if the food we relished so much as youngsters would taste the same today. It might be like Daddy and the apple dumplings.

He took a hankering for some of Grandma's boiled apple dumplings — the kind you boil in water until they turn sort of blue and gummy. He kept on until Mom finally made him some. He eagerly scooped out a nice fat one, put it in a bowl and added sugar and milk. After a bite or two, he remarked with something less than enthusiasm, "These don't taste like Mommy's." Mom just grinned. Later she told me that they did so taste like Grandma's. Hers weren't fit to eat either!

When we were kids, we would eat anything. Mom would dump a lot of leftovers in a skillet, add a chopped onion and a jar of canned tomatoes, and stew it all together. We called it "slumgullion" and ate it with gusto. We downed cookers of "flapdoodle" or blackberries well sweetened and thickened with cornstarch, which we ate with hot biscuits and lots of butter. It was unheard of for a kid to go to the table and say, "I don't like anything you have!" A pot of boiled potatoes and a hunk of corn bread tasted wonderful when you came in the house, cold and famished.

I grew up on real cow butter that we churned ourselves in an old fashioned churn with a wooden dasher and lid. I loved that butter, but I hated to churn. Mom didn't like to heat the milk too much, as it made white butter, and sometimes the butter wouldn't come, and then it wouldn't gather. We would have to set the whole churn down in a dishpan of warm water to get the milk the right temperature so the butter would gather to the top. If you didn't pay attention to what you were doing, (and I was usually reading a book) the dasher would slip sideways and throw a shower of buttermilk from head to foot. Mom liked to "take up" the butter herself, but sometimes she would let one of us older girls wash it for her. This involved change after change of cold water until the final one ran perfectly clear. I remember washing the butter one day and draining off the water by pouring it over the banister on the back porch. Daydreaming as usual, I let the whole bowl of butter slide out on the muddy ground with a wet splat. Needless to say, I wasn't too popular with Mom for awhile.

We were amply paid for our efforts when Mom

would set the big pan of golden brown biscuits on the table to go with the yellow butter we had churned. To top it off, we had honey from our own honey bees that Daddy robbed periodically. We just take for granted now that we can go in the supermarket and grab a gallon of milk, but back then we knew the source of our food and the effort it took to produce it.

We seemed to work much harder then, but we also seemed to have more leisure time. Evenings brought simple games that we thoroughly enjoyed such as "Fistalk" and "Hully-Gully" which was played with kernels of field corn. For snacks, someone went to the cellar and got a bowl of apples, or we popped some corn in an old iron skillet. It seems that the more labor saving devices we have, the less time we have to enjoy life.

The Clay Free Press
December 8, 1982

The fire feels warm and comforting at night; it is a good time for the family to gather around for popcorn and homemade cookies, and tales of long ago. I loved these evenings when I was a little girl and Daddy told us stories. He was a master story teller and had many rich experiences to draw from. He was twenty-seven before he married and settled down, and had "hoboed" out west twice during the depression, joining the thousands and thousands of unemployed men who "rode the rails" at that time. We shivered with him as he recounted riding across the plains, cold and hungry, in an open boxcar. Our indignation rose when a muscular storekeeper picked him up by the scruff of the neck and the seat of his pants and threw him out of the store when he asked for a handout crying, "We don't allow no bums in here!" We camped out in a hobo jungle with him and made mulligan stew, and eagerly opened the big package that a butcher had given him to find a whole hog skin. We shared Daddy's chagrin, and the other men's joy, as they eagerly jumped in and began cutting hunks of it for beans and stew. We heard the hobo scream as he caught his foot in the couplings of a train, and saw one man fall off in a Colorado gorge. We panned gold one winter with him, and at this point he always got out the little cloth pouch of gold dust that he had collected.

It was only after he had his stroke that he told us that many of the hobo tales were embellishments, and I was oddly deflated. All my life I had believed them as gospel truth. Fact and fantasy were so intermingled by then that not even he could separate them.

Then Mom would tell us about her life on Big Laurel Creek when she was a girl. Many people will tell you today that it was easier back then to raise a dozen kids than it is to raise two now. I don't think "easier" is the right word. Grandma and Grandpa Samples had eleven children to provide for; her day began at four in the morning when she got up to build fires and cook breakfast. The older boys were rousted out about five. Grandma had to milk and do the feeding of the livestock, and sometimes the girls had to milk, too. Even the little ones got out of bed by six o'clock, and the day had begun. If it was wash day, Grandma had to carry the water, heat it on the stove, and go at it with wash tub and wash board. I wonder how many of us modern mothers could walk in Grandma's footsteps? No wonder they sewed the kid's long-johns on for the winter! Grandpa and the older boys would go to the cornfields or to cut wood, and the school children had a two mile walk to school. She would describe the boy's high topped shoes that the girls also wore in the winter, which always split down the back before winter was over, and the cold and snow that they had to trek through. We would pull our chairs a little closer to the fire and wrap our feedsack gowns tighter around us, and feel that we were the luckiest children alive.

The Clay Free Press
November 4, 1981

We took a couple of days off this week and journeyed to the land of Old Ed and the booby owls, or the Jackson County farm where we lived so long ago, and no one has lived in since. But it was like a scarce-remembered dream that hovers barely in the memory — almost as if we had never lived there. There is something pitiful about an old farmstead falling apart, and ours was no exception. The main part of the old, white, two-story house stood firm, but the kitchen had fallen down in a tangle of rotten boards and torn linoleum. The "Wallrite" wallpaper had peeled away in strips, exposing the old newspapers that had been pasted on the bare boards. One paper was dated 1941. The matched flooring on the main part was solid as ever, but the chimney had fallen down and blocked the stairway and front door. The front porch that once ran the whole width of the house had fallen completely down, giving a forlorn and complete surrender to the ravages of time. The front yard was grown up in a welter of vines and underbrush, and the chipyard where we once cut our wood was a forest of walnut trees. The big barn was standing still, a silent gray ghost, although the cellar house was gone. Only the square stones of the cellar remained, overgrown with briers and weeds. The two room outbuilding we had used for a shop and tool house still stubbornly stood. This was a farm that had once known children, joys and sorrows, was tilled and harvested — a home for families who lived, loved and died. The only thing that remained unchanged was the enormous stone step beside the front porch. Untouched by time, it keeps a lonely vigil at this deserted old farmhouse.

The only trace we left behind to show that we had ever lived there was the little bed that Criss had made for Michael; its broken springs and torn mattress had provided countless nests for field mice and was lying beside the handmade stead.

Time continues its relentless march onward; ever-changing and never stopping. We are swept along with the tide of time. How sad it would be if all we mortals had to look forward to was to grow old, decay, and fall down like these abandoned houses. The apostle Paul said in I Corinthians 15:19: "If in this life only we have hope in Christ, we are of all men most miserable." Thank God for a hope that goes beyond the decay of this life.

The Clay Free Press
November 11, 1981

A thin, honking cry sounds from the vast reaches of the November sky; the plaintive farewell of the wild goose as he disappears over the horizon. A lone house cricket plays a mournful melody in the corner of the cellar, and the birdsong that once poured from a thousand throats has dwindled to a solitary note now and then. It's the lonesomest sound of all, bidding summer a last good-bye.

The saddest sound I have ever heard is the lonely cry of a train whistle in the night. When the

136

trains used to run up Camp Creek, and the weather conditions were just right, the sound would carry all the way up our holler. That faraway whistle in the night would cause shivers to run up and down my spine and create a vague sadness in my heart. It would make me think of places I had never been, and would never be, and people I had never met, and would never meet. Mom would quote an old poem, only part of which I remember. It goes like this —

"Far, far, lost and gone, the train went over the hill,
Rise up and cry, against the starry sky,
Turn again as the echoes die,
And tear me as you will.
I think I could go my quiet way,
And be silent all through the years,
Were it not for that lonely cry in the night,
And my lonely, answering tears."

Then I snuggle up in my nice warm bed beside my sleeping husband, and count my blessings (all sleeping in their nice warm beds) and I am glad I am who I am and where I am.

The Clay Free Press
November 18, 1981

We burned a barn full of memories last night. My brother Larry had called some time before, asking me if I cared if he tore the old barn down. I had no objections; it had been unused for several years and was beginning to fall down anyway. He went on to say that he wanted to save the hand-hewn logs to build a room on his fishing camp at William's River, and that way the logs would be preserved. He added that he was sort of sentimental about the old barn where we played so much in days gone by.

I got to thinking about how much time we did spend in play there; next to the woods, it was our favorite place to play. It was never a pretty edifice, although it was extremely solid. The main part was built of heavy logs that came out of an old log cabin, with two stalls built on and a shed on the side. There was an upper story over all of this where the hay was stored to the ceiling. We never had our hay baled then, and it was a perfect hideout for a gang of kids. Daddy would tell us sternly not to jump on the hay, as the cows didn't relish it too much when we tromped around on it. Of course the temptation was too much, and we would sneak and play in it anyway.

One of our favorite games was to climb up the ladder to the loft, crawl across the hay, and jump out the upper story window. This would be repeated over and over with us lined up like a bunch of fledgling paratroopers waiting for the jump. This sounds like sheer torture to me now, but then it was great fun. We played cops and robbers, cowboys and Indians, and sometimes the whole barn was a huge pirate ship afloat on boundless seas.

We formed a secret club and our club house was the barn. We saved our money in a glass jar, and we had a quarter (contributed by Alen Wayne, the only rich member in our club) and some pennies scraped up by the rest of us. I wonder what happened to our funds when the club disbanded? I strongly suspect that it went for the jar of marshmallow cream that Larry and Coda climbed up on the Virginia office porch roof to eat — taunting the rest of us.

In the spring Daddy would let us girls clean out one stall for a play house. The manger full of hay made a perfect bed, and sometimes the boys could be bribed to play house with us. We carried old dishes and cookers there, and mixed clay mud and water to make wonderful pies and mud-cakes. Once I made a beautiful pokeberry pie, and cut Larry a wedge. He got so carried away that he took a great bite out of it.

As I look back now, I realize that we spent many of our days there, and the boys spent lots of their nights. It was sort of like camping out, only conveniently close to home. When Peggy Ann and I were in high school, we decided one night to sleep in the barn. It was late fall, and we felt quite daring as we trailed a blanket apiece and climbed the ladder to the loft. We burrowed back in the hay, each in her own blanket, and felt nice and cozy. Along in the night the temperature dropped, the frost fell, and I woke up freezing to death. "Peggy Ann," I chattered," "Get up and let's lie on your blanket and cover up with mine." She co-operated, but I'll never forget her sleepy comment, "Take up thy bed and walk."

I reckon we just burned the barn. The memories are still there.

The Clay Free Press
December 2, 1981
The Charleston Gazette
March 28, 1991

A balmy wind rattles the few remaining chestnut leaves in the top of the big tree at the edge of the yard and makes a sighing sound through the bare limbs of the sycamore. Most of the trees have been divested of their autumn finery, and stand in stark beauty with their naked limbs silhouetted against the November sky. It has been such a short time since we saw the new buds begin to swell, then form velvety, infant leaves. Almost before our eyes, they grew full-blown and mature; swiftly changing to the brilliant riot of autumn's colors. Now they lie, brown and spent, to nourish the soil for next year's crops, and thus the cycle of life begins again.

There is a perceptible change in the weather this morning. Yesterday was one of those rare, mild days that November sometimes offers, with warm sunshine and blue smoky shadows that nestle in each cove and holler. While I was out raking the yard, I came upon a coal black wooly-worm without a trace of white anywhere. I think he was trying to tell me something — perhaps it was simply to enjoy the lovely day, as they will be few and far between now.

This is the time of year that we used to have our pie socials at Hagar School. Sometimes called a box and pie social, it has become a thing of the past. Not only was it a money-making project for the school, it was a social event eagerly looked forward to by the young people. We also had an Ugly Man and Pretty Girl contest, along with a cakewalk or two (I wonder now how many times someone was conked in the head, accidently on purpose, by that broomstick?) The pies were the main attraction, however. Each girl and young woman made their fanciest pie, and decorated a box to conceal the contents. I'm afraid that many times more time was spent decorating the box than making the pie. These were to be raffled off anonymously to the boys and young men, but of course the girls who had steady boy friends dropped a hint as to which box was theirs, which created some fast and furious bidding.

The first one I was allowed to take part in was when I was a scrawny kid of twelve or so. Mom made a delicious homemade caramel pie, and this time she decided to embellish it — which was gilding the lily, anyway. She added extra butter and sugar, then topped it off with a high, glossy meringue. I spent hours trimming a box in blue and white crepe paper, garnished with ruffles and ribbons. Time for the pie social came, and we watched the pies being raffled off; one by one. My heart beat furiously when my blue and white box was held up high and bid on. It was bought by a young man by the name of Bob Rogers, and I can imagine his chagrin when he discovered it belonged to a little twelve-year-old girl. It was customary to sit with the boy who bought your pie, and we squeezed together in an old school desk. To my utter embarrassment, Mom's famous pie had turned to the consistency of melted ice cream and ran all over the pie pan when we cut it. Bob was the soul of kindness and tried to cover my humiliation by remarking that the pie was delicious and we would just eat it with a spoon. Bob was one of America's many boys who marched away to fight on foreign soil and never came home again. But after all these years, I still remember the ruddy-cheeked boy who was so kind and considerate to a skinny little girl.

The Clay Free Press
November 17, 1982

Our first killing frost came silently in the night, touching our hills with chilly fingers. We awoke to a white garment of death spread over our flowers and gardens, leaving a trail of black and broken plants behind. The scarlet sage and cockscomb stand with bent and withered heads; their color drained and their glory gone. The sweet pepper plants are blasted and spent; frostbitten peppers clinging to their frozen stems. The rising sun brings out the sharp, acrid smell of frostbite, testifying that the garden is really gone at last.

The last of the fall chores are wrapped up for

the winter. I cleaned out the chicken house this week, and thought that this is one aspect of our memories that are sometimes forgotten as we reminisce. Just like the outhouse of yesteryear, there is a seamier side to country living that we sometimes gloss over. We had to clean out barns and chicken houses, and scatter the manure on the gardens. Everything about the farm wasn't necessarily rose gardens. It used to be my job to go after the cows in the evening, and bring them to the barn to be milked. I would walk behind them, daydreaming, until the soft splat-splat in front of my feet would bring me back to earth.

Mom and my granddaughter, Chrissie, were out in the pasture field a few weeks ago hunting ripe pawpaws. Chrissie has spent her tender years in the state of Louisiana, and farm living is completely new to her. "Mom-Granny, what is this soft stuff that I am walking in?" she asked. She was more interested than revolted when Mom explained to her about cow patties and the facts of life.

Our way of life is probably strange to the natives of other states. I got a letter from a cousin who was transplanted from the hills of West Virginia to the lake region of Michigan, and he says, "I found the natives here to be rather stiff and cold at first contact. Store clerks are just short of rude, and very few understand southern humor. After getting acquainted, I find them warm and generous. But they have never heard of cooking beans in a pot with a ham hock. They make baked beans. They know nothing about pickled corn, copperheads, pawpaws, gooseberries, or slaw on hot dogs."

A land of no brown beans or pickled corn? Do you reckon they know they are deprived?

The Clay Free Press
November 7, 1984

In a last minute gesture of good will, November tossed us a few days of mild weather before departing. Frosty mornings turned to sunny days, as she threw us the last kiss of summer before the stark reality of winter in the hills begins.

It gave us time to take one more long walk in the woods before cold weather, so Criss and I took advantage of the opportunity. We went up the "little road" past the old Butler farm, climbed the hill past the barn, and went on up through the woods where the present owners are now clearing. The dry pine needles crunched underfoot, and piles of neatly stacked underbrush gave evidence of much hard labor. Mrs. Smith told us that while they were clearing a flat there, they discovered an old, old cemetery with stones for markers. She took us to the foot of a big oak tree, where the graves were laid out in parallel rows with head and foot stones marking each grave. There were no names on the stones; forgotten people from a forgotten day. They had carefully cleared the brush and debris from the whole area, leaving the graves plainly visible. Trailing myrtle vine grew rampant underfoot; mute evidence that someone once cared and remembered. It gave me an eerie feeling to stand there and look at those forgotten, unmarked graves on a lonely West Virginia hillside, and realize that these were once real people who had lived, had hopes and dreams, joys and sorrows; now nobody knows or cares. I have lived here all my life and wasn't aware of the existence of this cemetery. Whether you are buried in a stately mausoleum, or in an isolated grave marked by two rough stones, we all come down to the same level in death.

Ecclesiastes 9:5-6 says, "For the living know that they shall die; but the dead know not anything, neither have they any more a reward; for the memory

of them is forgotten, Also their love and their hatred, and their envy, is now perished; neither have they any more a portion for ever in anything that is done under the sun."
And there they lie until Judgement Day.
The Clay Free Press
December 5, 1984

The warm, spicy smell of pumpkin pies, the mouthwatering aroma of the brown turkey liberally stuffed with onion-sage dressing, the yeasty goodness of hot rolls rising high and puffy — these are the smells of Thanksgiving. The excited chatter of the little ones, the contented murmur of conversation among the older generation, sudden bursts of laughter coming from the kitchen — these are the sounds of the season. The satisfying closeness of family ties, the genuine love that radiates from heart to heart, the multitude of precious memories of Thanksgivings past — these are the emotions of the day. Thanksgiving is all of this, and more. More than the smells, more than the sounds, much more than the family love that glows so brightly — even more than the emotions that are entwined in the heart strings.

Thanksgiving is not just a day, but a way of life — a deep gratitude to God every day for all of His many blessings. I am glad that America has set this day aside for a special day of giving thanks. How could anyone celebrate this day and not acknowledge the great God of all heavens?

The mind naturally strays back to the past, and holidays spent with loved ones now gone. When I was little, we never had turkey, but Mom would stuff and roast a couple of fat chickens. She would bake a table full of cakes and pies, and our eyes would pop out at all the goodies laid out before us. I can see Grandpa O'Dell take his place at the head of the table, with Daddy beside him, and all the young'ens crowded on the bench behind. We would bow our heads while the blessing was said, fidgeting impatiently as we waited for the last amen.

Grandpa loved to eat. He wouldn't wear his store bought teeth, but he could eat anything he wanted. I can still hear him telling Mom, "Fetch up some more bread." He liked his taters "b'iled," and talked about the baby being "sp'iled," but he was he one who sp'iled all the babies. He was a short man, something over five and a half feet tall, but he stood straight as a ramrod. He loved having his picture taken, and would take a Napoleon-like stance with one hand in his bosom and a stern look on his face. I can remember his testimony at church, "When God ran me through His sawmill, He had to knock off a lot of bumps and knots. I came out as a two by four, but I was straight!" he would say.

He would journey alone on a Greyhound bus to various parts of the country, although he couldn't read. He made his home with us for ten years, and we were always so tickled to see him return home from one of his visits to relatives in Oregon. He would set his black "grip" down and begin rummaging through it for the apples and candy he invariably brought back to us. He would look up with a scowl on his face and say in mock ferocity, "Git out of here now, I ain't got nothin' fer ye — jist a little bit fer your Mammy!" After we had family prayer at night, I would go to sleep hearing Grandpa repeat his prayers in a loud stage whisper, "Lord we thank You for this beautiful sunshine day." He was such a good grandfather — I loved him and miss him still.

Daddy loved our family gatherings. He liked to

make the salads, and leaned heavy on black olives and lots of cheese. If he made a fruit salad, it had to have chopped raw apple in it. There are so many memories, some of them not so good. Daddy spent his last Thanksgiving in a nursing home, and only those who have walked this path know the special heartache that goes along with this. (Don't ever say that you will never do this — you don't know what time will bring to you.) But the good memories far outweigh the bad. I'm so thankful that the Lord heals the heartaches and dims the bad memories with the passing of time, but lets the good memories glow ever brighter.

The Clay Free Press
November 24, 1982

"What makes happiness, Lord?"

Benji, Jessica and Joseph are seated around the kitchen table. They are chopping nuts for the pound cake; three brown heads bent intently over their task . . . the kitchen is warm and cozy; the air full of the fragrance of cinnamon, ginger and cloves as pumpkin pies bake in the oven . . . the grandchildren are "helping" to prepare the holiday food; eagerly they tackle each assigned task . . . Joseph's brown eyes sparkle as he pops an occasional nut in his mouth . . . he grins and remarks, "Mommaw, if we weren't here, you wouldn't have anyone to lick the bowl and beaters, would you?"

Outside, the snow spats against the windowpane and turns the lawn into an ever-increasing whiteness. There is warmth and cheer in the kitchen, and close companionship between grandchildren and grandmother. My heart is blessed as I hand them the bowl and mixer beaters to lick.

"Is this what makes happiness, Lord?"

The men are late from their hunting trip. They have been gone since Sunday, and all day I have watched the road for them. Snow falls heavier as darkness approaches; it is beginning to lie on the road, and I am uneasy. Each set of approaching headlights sends me hurrying to the window — but each vehicle passes the house and goes on by . . .

With a sudden burst of cold air, the front door is flung open and the hunters are home. Full of laughter and robust good humor, they fill the house with their hunting gear, their hunting tales, and their presence. I suddenly realize how empty my week has been without my tall grown sons wandering in and out of the house, and how incomplete I am without my "other half."

"Is my happiness made up of this, Lord?"

The night wears on, but I cannot sleep. My oldest daughter and her family are traveling on this slippery road tonight. I miss her so much; this tall daughter of mine. She lived in sight of us all her married life, until a few weeks ago when they moved out of state where her husband had found employment. It is a five hour drive home, and I can visualize the car, with the three boisterous little boys, sliding on the treacherous highway and going out of control . . .

I sleep fitfully, and then I awaken to the sound of a door opening and footsteps across the floor. They have arrived! Someone described her recently as a "breath of fresh air" — she is that and more. Although it is not daylight, we get up, cook breakfast together, talking a mile a minute; trying to cram the last few week's events into the first hour. It is so good to have her home.

"Is my happiness based on this, Lord?"

The turkey reigns over the full table; brown and

plump and steaming with onion-sage dressing. The pumpkin pies are picture-perfect; from the relish tray to the cranberry sauce to the crusty hot rolls the table is complete. My heart swells to the bursting point as brown and blonde heads bow in thanksgiving for our blessings . . . my thoughts go to the baby of the family who is spending the day with her in-laws this year . . . the oldest son and his family celebrating at home with her parents . . . still part of the family circle.

"Surely this is my happiness, Lord."

Night falls softly; the hustle and bustle of the day is stilled. The good memories of the day linger on, warming my meditations. How can I say, "Thank you, Lord" for all of these blessings? Yes, I know what makes happiness, Lord. It is the thread of love that comes from You and wraps around each heart and binds us together. From parents to children to grandchildren, back and forth, it weaves a chain of love that has its beginning and ending in you, Lord. It is strengthened through our happy times together, and nurtured through our memories. Through good times and bad, it is Your love that holds us together.

Thank you, Lord, for your gift of love to us.

The Clay Herald
December 4, 1989

A bitter wind whistles through the bare limbs of the trees and sends scattered snowflakes through the air. The unaccustomed cold drives us into the house and makes us doubly thankful for the warm, glowing fire. Through the window, I can see the hemlocks on the bank shivering in the cold. The hills, solid and unmovable, face the onslaught of winter weather with their brown shoulders braced against the cold. I love these hills. I wonder if you have to be born and bred here to love them as fiercely as I do.

I love the hills in the autumn when God paints the trees in colors too rich for any artist to portray, and the feeble tongue of a poet could never describe. My soul sings when Indian summer comes to the land, and the morning mist hangs bluish on the mountain tops. It is almost too much to take in when the woodsmoke hangs in the air like a half-forgotten memory that strikes a deep chord in the heart. I love it when November colors the hills in monochrome shades of gray and brown — gray skies and grayer rain; brown fields and browner leaves.

When winter coats the hills in robes of snowy white, nothing can be more beautiful. The trees stand with outstretched arms, clothed with the brilliance of diamonds. The creek comes to a standstill; frozen in the very act of flowing, and on each tiny twig dipped in the water, there shines a crystal bell. Spring is a glorious season, ushered in by fickle March, who can't decide whether to "go spring or stay winter." I love those first warm spring days when the tiny wild flowers begin appearing among the dead leaves of winter, and the tender young mountain tea leaves wait to be picked.

Summer brings maturity to our hills, with the trees festooned with their full blown leaves, and the earth rampant with growth. It is a busy time, with crops and gardens. But autumn comes and summer is over — and winter comes again.

The Clay Free Press
November 16, 1983

WHEN THE WIND COMES WHISTLIN'

November tucks her brown robes around her and departs swiftly, clearing the way for snowflakes and the icy winds of December. December is a sparkling month, especially for the children, filled with holiday excitement: snowballs and sleigh rides, carols and Christmas.

December wears a definite fragrance — compounded of crisp, cold air, the piney scent of evergreens, warm candle wax, and the cinnamony smell of fresh-baked cookies. She travels these hills in a long white gown, with snowflakes in her hair and frost sparkling underfoot.

Her voice is sweet and musical: echoing Christmas carols and silver bells, joyous shouts of red-cheeked children, and the soft spat of snow against the window pane. December sparkles with snow-sprinkled hemlocks; her nighttime sky is filled with a myriad of stars that seem to glow bigger and brighter than at any other time of the year. Her colors contrast sharply, in the flash of a red cardinal against her snowy slopes, and in the bright crimson holly berries clustered against the green of its leaves. Her voice is a little sharper in the chill wind that howls around the eaves and comes shrieking through the bare branches of the trees.

We greet her with mixed emotions, for her appearance means that our outdoor days in the mild fall temperatures are over for the year. Still, it is cozy in the house, with the wood fire burning bright, and these cold days give us time to read and sew; quilt or visit.

The first snowflakes are appearing, and I find myself dragging out the soup cooker. A kettle full of beef stew is simmering on the stove, ready for the horde of hunters who will descend upon me before this day is over. I will make a pone of cornbread in my biggest iron skillet, and that is supper.

The Clay Herald

December 12, 1988

A capricious wind is blowing this morning, rustling through the pines on the hill and rattling the dead weeds along the creek bank. It hurries the heavy, dark clouds overhead without mercy, and under its mild, almost balmy demeanor, there sounds a sinister note of worse to come. A solitary bird nest perched on the limb of the chestnut tree sways to and fro, the former resident having gone to warmer climes months ago.

The winter days are a respite from the more rushed months of the year. These slower paced days are ideal for cleaning out the accumulation in dresser drawers, browsing through old papers, and reminiscing through old snapshots. Grandpa used to call this "plundering around."

The flu bug that bit me awhile back has left me with a hacking cough that has settled in like a permanent resident. My son-in-law recommends boiling some yellow root and pine needles together for a cough syrup which he says is a sure cure, but I haven't tried it yet. For one thing, I wasn't sure what kind of pine needles to use. Blue spruce? Scotch? Wasn't it a cup of hemlock that Socrates quaffed and was never bothered with a cough again? Would you recommend this to your mother-in-law?

My own mother-in-law used to make a cough syrup that really did work. Along with the yellow root, she used black oak bark, slippery elm bark, and honey. I wish I had paid more attention and written down the ingredients and measurements she used. Some of these old remedies were quite effective. I

know that yellow root, or goldenseal, is one of the best
medicines for a sore throat that you can use, but it is
bitter. Grandma O'Dell was well-versed in the usage
of plants and herbs, and I wish she had passed the
knowledge down to some of us. I recognize
pennyroyal, and old field balsam (how many of you
have chewed that?) horse mint, and of course,
peppermint. We used to chew strips of slippery elm
and the tender sprouts of sassafras. I can recognize
pipsissewa, although I don't know what it is used for,
and coltsfoot. But I wish I knew lots more. You never
know when you might have to fall back on your own
resources to survive.

The Clay Free Press
January 12, 1983

The echoes from our hills and valleys are
muffled today by the snow that came silently in the
night. It has continued all through the day, covering
field and hillside alike with a fluffy white coat. The
hemlocks on the roadbank lift heavy limbs encrusted
with snow jewels, and the bare limbs on the sycamores
are festooned with white velvet. A pair of cardinals
and a dozen or so juncos search the creek bank for
food, their tiny wings flickering from limb to limb. A
black-capped chickadee and a male cardinal stand out
against the whiteness of the snow, and there is a mad
scramble for the bran and cracked corn in the bird
feeder.

Yesterday dawned clear and bright, with no hint
of the snow that was forecast. There was not a cloud
to mar the blueness of the sky, and the sun streamed
down brightly, turning the broom sage patch on the
hill to dull gold. When we were kids, we loved to play
hide-and-seek in the fields of broom sage. I remember

someone telling me then that our old Clay County farm wouldn't raise anything except O'Dell's and broom sage. I was insulted.

The wind picks up the snow and splats it against the kitchen window, but inside it is warm and cheery. A pot of chili bubbles on the stove and sends out an enticing, spicy smell. This is a day to stay indoors, pop a big bowl of popcorn, and play a game of checkers or dominos. We have been doing some reading aloud at night. Right now we are in the middle of "Where the Red Fern Grows," by Wilson Rawls. It almost makes me want to start coon hunting. Reading together is one of the best ways to bring a family closer. Daddy used to read to us by the hour.

I can close my eyes and feel myself back home again in the old Jenny Lind house, with the wind howling at the windows and creeping through the cracks. The gas heater is turned up high, and we children are sprawled on chairs pulled up close to Daddy, or lying on the floor at his feet. I can hear the tone of his voice spilling out chapter after chapter of Don Fendler, the little boy who was lost in the western mountains many years ago. He loved to read us stories of when the west was settled, and could tell stories more interesting than those that came from a book. The ones I remember best were the Bible stories. Daddy had the knack of making the stories come alive, and when he would tell us about Joseph, the little Israelite boy who was taken from his family and sold into slavery down in Egypt, we would shed many tears. Daddy would choke up and cry along with us. Then it would be time to read the Bible and have prayer. Many, many times we would go to sleep down on our knees. I loved that secure feeling of being tucked in bed at night and hearing the children call back and forth, "Good-night Daddy, I love you;

Good-night Mommy, I love you; Good-night Alyce Faye, I love you; Good-night Larry, I love you; Good-night Mary Ellen, I love you; Good-night Mark, I love you; Good-night Ronnie, I love you; Good-night Jeannie, I love you; Good-night Susie, I love you." This was repeated back and forth until every child had a turn, and by then it was almost time to get up.

Right up until the time that Daddy lost his speech, just a few days before God called him home, Daddy would say to me when I told him good-bye, "Good-bye, Alyce Faye, I love you." Someday I'll tell him, "Hello Daddy, I still love you."

Take time with your children, read to them, tell them stories and love them. We have them such a short time, and then they are gone. The foundation we lay and the memories we make will last a lifetime.

The Clay Free Press
January 19, 1983

A fine misty rain, that threatens at any minute to turn to snow, is falling on the ground. The sky is dark and threatening, and the woodsmoke from the chimney spirals downward toward the ground. Outside it is cold and gloomy, but the kitchen is warm and comforting, and fragrant with the gingery smell of molasses cookies in the oven.

Christmas looms closer, and parents are shopping for every conceivable toy that can be imagined. Millions of dollars are being spent on toys for this season, and yet I wonder if children today have any more fun with these expensive things than we used to have with the homemade gadgets that Daddy made. Of course we had "bought" toys at Christmas, but it's funny that I can't remember them nearly as well as I do the whirligigs carved out of a wooden thread spool and fitted with a pointed stick. In the summer, Daddy made whistles out of elderberry stalks, and popguns that would burn a blister. We would string a button on a thread and make a "hummer," and how it did hurt when someone wound up your hair in it. A discarded alarm clock gave us hours of play — tiny whirligigs that we raced to see whose would spin the longest. When Criss was young, he made miniature sawmills out of clock parts. We girls spent hours playing with paper dolls that Mom drew for us, drawing and cutting out dresses. Somehow the dresses cut from the Sears and Roebuck catalog never fit just right — there would be an arm or leg positioned wrong. It has been many a year since I have seen a homemade paper doll. I almost wish I could reach under my bed and pull out the box of paper dolls and play with them once again.

Time goes on, and my days of play are over. But somehow I wish it would hold still just for a little bit and let my granddaughters play a little longer than I did.

The Clay Free Press
December 14, 1983

Grandpa Huge wrote to us many years ago early in December, and his opening sentence was, "This is Christmas month." I have a vivid memory of his fluffy, white beard, and kind eyes that twinkled. I remember the little one room log cabin where he spent his remaining days all alone, and the clock on the shelf that ticked away the hours.

As we were leaving one day after a visit, he handed me a large hunk of warm batter bread, liberally spread with white cow butter and sprinkled with sugar. As we climbed the hill back to the car, the butter dripped off my elbows and the sugar ran down my chin. I thought it was the most delicious food I had ever eaten.

This was a frantic month back in Hagar School. When Mr. Hinkle was principal, we always put on an elaborate Christmas program for the whole community. Our preparations began early in November, and each child in school had to participate. We would have two or three long plays, plus poems, skits, and songs. Mr. Hinkle was an exacting director, and we had to have our parts memorized, and also put the right "feeling" into it. We would troop down to the Methodist Church every afternoon for weeks preceding Christmas to go through the entire program.

There was such excitement the night of the program. People would come for miles to see it, and there would hardly be parking room for all the vehicles. Our family would walk to the church, and I can still hear the squeaky crunch of the snow underfoot, see the stars twinkling overhead, and feel the excitement rising to a fever pitch, making it hard to breathe or even think.

The church would be so crowded that latecomers would have to stand in the aisles. We would rush around behind closed curtains, pinning on costumes and putting last minute props together, with the sinking feeling that we would forget our parts, for certain. One time just before the program began, Avis June lifted my baby brother, Ronnie, up high to see the crowd. He got scared and grabbed the wire holding the curtains with both hands, and down it all came. A red-faced Mr. Hinkle rushed up, exclaiming disgustedly, "I knew that doggoned nail wouldn't hold!" We never did tell him that Ronnie pulled it down.

There were many factors involved that we didn't think of as children. One was the extreme generosity of the people at the Methodist Church in letting us use their building for weeks to practice, and another was how much we benefitted from the whole program. We acquired some much needed self confidence in learning to speak before a crowd, we learned teamwork in putting on a play together, and we also learned to memorize. I can still remember some of the poems that the other kids recited.

Mr. Hinkle could have had another motive in keeping us busy all those weeks that time of year. We didn't have swings, slides, and playground equipment such as the schools have now. We had a dirt playground, and before the ground froze real hard, it would be a muddy mess. The boys always found a good, sloppy mudbank to slide in, and sometimes their blue jeans would be so mud covered that you couldn't tell what color they were. We didn't have much to entertain us until sleigh riding weather came, and our Christmas program kept us busy until then.

December — it is still a special month. It is a perfect time for families to get together, to express appreciation, to show love. The things we are doing now will be the memories we look back upon. Let's make them good memories.

The Clay Free Press
December 9, 1981
The Charleston Gazette
December 13, 1991
The Clay Herald
December 9, 1991

Winter entered our hills and valleys like a raging fury, bringing icy winds, frigid air, and snow that kept falling. All the wishes for a white Christmas were granted as Christmas Eve found many people stranded by the snow that came quickly and unexpectedly. Bitter cold air flooded our hills as wailing winds whipped through the trees and howled around our houses. It lifted the swirling snow in blinding waves and quickly drove to shelter all the barnyard animals. Life was reduced to keeping the livestock warm and fed, as well as ourselves. Our day consisted of feeding chunks of wood to the wood stove, and stopping every chink that the wind could creep through. The wind chill factor was thirty below zero.

As we sat around a roaring fire, we discussed how the oldtimers managed to keep warm during the cold winter months. As the day wore on, however, and water pipes kept freezing and bursting all around us, I was inclined to believe that they could survive a cold spell better than we do. After all, with no indoor plumbing, there were no pipes to freeze and burst. The pitcher pump that used to supply all of our watery needs gave out a gush of water no matter what the weather. And the two-holer that stood faithfully in the back yard never needed flushing. (Never mind the freezing trips that one had to make night and day; it was never out of commission.) When the water freezes off now, everything goes out of order. No baths — there are no washtubs hanging on the back porch for our weekly ablutions. I can tell you that the Saturday night bath at our house was no joke. We had a tin washpan that stood on a wash stand for our nightly needs, but the all-over, go-for-broke bath was reserved for Saturday night. If we had to pump our water by hand now, carry it in zinc buckets through wind and weather, heat it on the cookstove, and then pour it in a washtub, I'm afraid a lot of us wouldn't take a bath even once a week. I am still thankful every time I turn on the tap in the bathroom and hot, steaming water fills the tub — and I can stretch out my legs full length and not have to scrunch up in a washtub.

The children and grandchildren drifted in during the cold spell to gather around the fire and play games. Times may change, and games may change, but one thing never changes — that desire that our family has to get together on cold winter nights. When I was a kid, we played the old timey games that our parents had played, and told the same timeworn jokes and riddles over and over. Mom would take a turn reciting some of the countless poems that were stored in her head. I recall how her hands were always busy with sewing or mending even as she recited with feeling,

> When the wind comes a'whistlin'
> Cuttin' keen and sharp and shrill,
> And the snowflakes come a'driftin'
> In the valley and on the hill.
> And the air is full of Christmas,
> Then my mind goes back once more,
> To a little old log cabin,
> On Virginny's sunny shore.

On and on her voice would hum, while the wind outside whistled around our own little shack. Sometimes she would sing the mournful tunes of old, of Barb'ry Ellen and Sweet William and how "On William's grave, there grew a red rose; On Barb'ry's grew a green brier. Oh, they grew to the top of the old church door, 'til they couldn't grow any higher, then they wrapped and they twined in a true lover's knot, and the rose grew 'round the brier...". Daddy would sing, "Huckleberry pie and blackberry puddin' and I'd give it all away, just to hug Sally Gooden!"

The wind wails around my house tonight with a crying sound as it blows through the eaves. It seems as if, from long ago and far away, I can hear the echo of Daddy's voice, "In the sweet bye and bye, we shall

meet on that beautiful shore."
The Clay Free Press
January 4, 1984

When Christmas time came, Daddy would go out in the woods and cut the most perfect tree he could find, and it was always so tall that he would have to trim the top to fit it in the old-fashioned high ceiling of our front room. Each ornament and glass ball had to be hung with precision, and each strand of tinsel had to be separated and spaced carefully on every bough. He was lord and master of that tree, and we didn't contribute a whole lot to the trimming of it — although one of the babies once tried to eat a glass ball. One memorable night Daddy fell out of the top of it while he was perched on a ladder trimming the top limbs.

We anxiously counted the days, in a fever of anticipation, until the night before Christmas finally came. And that was the best time to me. Daddy would gather us around the fire, with the baby cuddled on his lap, and read to us the story of the birth of Jesus from the Bible. We could hear the spattering of snow on the window outside, and the cold wind howling around the windowsills. We felt so snug and warm, clad in our feedsack gowns, listening to Daddy's voice as he read.

"And it came to pass in those days, that there went out a decree from Caesar Augustus, that all the world should be taxed. And this taxing was first made when Cyrenius was governor of Syria. And all went to be taxed, everyone into his own city." In our imagination, we could see the legions of Roman soldiers, marching the highways, enforcing the decree of taxation — and the crowds of common people, traveling to the city of their birth to pay their taxes.

"And Joseph also went up from Galilee, out of the city of Nazareth, unto the city of David, which is called Bethlehem: (because he was of the house and lineage of David) to be taxed with Mary his espoused wife, being great with child." The cold and snow would fade away, and we were there with Mary, plodding along on a little donkey on that hot, dusty road. (At least, it seemed to us that it should be hot in that desert country.) Mary was always clothed in a blue robe, and she was meek and uncomplaining.

"And so it was, that while they were there, the days were accomplished that she should be delivered." We knew about newborn babies . . . their tiny, innocent sweetness. With seven children, we had a little one most of the time — and we loved them.

"And she brought forth her firstborn son, and wrapped him in swaddling clothes, and laid him in a manger, because there was no room for them in the inn." We usually interrupted Daddy at this point to cry in high indignation, "How could they turn Jesus away? I would have let Him have my bed!" Although to us, the barn was not such a bad place; in fact, it was one of our favorite places to play. We could see the manger, filled with sweet-smelling hay, and that tiny baby wrapped in his swaddling clothes and peacefully sleeping. We could hear the placid cattle munching their feed and feel the body heat from them. We could see Mary and Joseph bending over him with love.

As Daddy finished the story, we were with the shepherds abiding in the fields, keeping watch over their flock by night. His voice would grow louder as he read, "And lo, the angel of the Lord came upon them, and the glory of the Lord shone round about them: and they were sore afraid." The boys had cows to tend themselves, and I am sure they identified with the frightened shepherds who had witnessed such a miracle.

"And the angel of the Lord said unto them, Fear not, for behold I bring you good tidings of great joy, which shall be to all people. For unto you is born a Savior, which is Christ the Lord." As he read on, we could see the multitude of heavenly host praising God and saying, "Glory to God in the highest, and on earth peace, good will toward men."

When I was little, it was just a beautiful story. It was only when I grew up and found the Lord in salvation that it became a reality in my life that brings joy every day of the year.

The Clay Herald
December 25, 1989

Thus we close out another year, and open the door for the new one. It dawns as bright and shining as the hope in a young child's eyes. The curtain of night is pulled back to reveal row upon row of slaty morning clouds, their edges ruffled and trimmed in deep rose. The colors change rapidly, and soon fade to pink streaks that grow dimmer and dimmer as morning emerges. The clouds dissipate, leaving the sky clear and blue, and the sun sparkles on the frosty hills. It is a beautiful beginning.

Closing the final page on a year causes the mind to reflect on the swift passage of time. It seems impossible that the year flew by so fast, and yet we stand on the threshold of another new year.

The Bible speaks of the brevity of our lives, describing our days on earth "as a shadow, and there is none abiding." Even when our lives are lengthened to the allotted three score and ten, or more, they are still but a "handbreadth." James says, "For what is your life? It is even a vapor, that appeareth for a little time, and then vanisheth away."

I saw this so plainly when Daddy lay on his death bed the last two days of his life. His speech was gone, but his eyes were as guileless and peaceful as a baby's, and they followed us in wonderment as we moved around the room. He was already entering that Eternal Place where time has no measure. I am sure, that if he could have spoken, he would have told us that "his days on this earth had been but a shadow." I watched him, and thought about his life. Everything he had tried to accomplish, and had accomplished, all his hopes, dreams and strivings — yes, and his failures, heartaches and disappointments, his family and friends, even his own life, meant nothing at all. The only thing that mattered was his soul and God. That is the point each one of us will come to, ready or not.

We look back on the past and wonder, what have we really accomplished? Many times we have failed — sometimes miserably. There is no use to mourn overlong for past mistakes. The saddest words on the tongue are, "Oh, if I could only go back and do that over!" This is like trying to gather up water that has been spilled on the ground. We need to use our stumbling blocks for stepping stones and look forward, not backward. It is also useless to worry about the future. Most of the things we worry about never come to pass, and real troubles usually come without warning.

Today — right now — is actually all the time we can claim. There may be many yesterdays in your life, but God does not promise tomorrow. At any age, the best thing a person can do is repent of their sins, forsake them, and walk in God's will for the remainder of their days — whether they be few or many. Then when we come to the place where it is just God and our soul, we can trustfully put our hand in the hand of our Savior and let Him lead us where time is no more.

"When I go to the grave I can say, as others have done, 'My day's work is done.' But I cannot say, 'My life is done.' My day's work will commence the next morning. The tomb is not a blind alley; it is a thoroughfare. It closes upon the twilight, but opens upon the dawn." — Victor Hugo

Our hills and hollers are still held in the deadly grip of winter, but now and then we get a glimpse of springtime to come. The snow has melted away leaving patches of startling green grass. Two pairs of flashy cardinals swoop out of the chestnut tree to feed on the cracked corn that has been placed there for them. They are joined by the smaller juncos, their snowy white breasts making a sharp contrast to their dark coats. Suddenly, they are all put to flight by a pair of lordly blue jays, who take over the feeder. It won't be long until their spring song fills the air and lifts our spirits.

We went down on Leatherwood last week. It was one of those foggy, misty mornings, almost like being in another world. The fog rolled and curled above the grove of jack pines, and was entangled in the bare branches of the birch and sycamore. Sheets of ice clung to the outcroppings of rocks on the roadside, and melting snow had raised the creek to a rush of greenish water. Rhododendron bushes crouched above the creek, and lacy hemlocks trailed graceful branches down to the rippling water beneath. It was easy to imagine how it will be later when the greening and blossoming touch of spring comes.

As I tried to fit six small grandsons behind my table on the back porch a few days ago, I thought with longing of the old bench we had at home when I was a kid. We had a big, homemade table covered with bright-checked oilcloth, and more kids than we had table. The bench was homemade too, and consisted of a straight back and a flat bottom. It was a rare meal when one of the kids didn't fall off the bench. Sometimes it happened while Daddy was asking the blessing — I figure many times there was a helping elbow. Daddy used to say he had to say grace with one eye open. This was not much of an exaggeration. I can see us now crowded around that old table. The babies learned early to run to Daddy to be fed, and they also learned not to put their hands in his plate. The grandbabies soon learned that it was Daddy who loved to feed them, but by the time the great-grandchildren came along, we were feeding Daddy.

Mom brought our food to the table in huge bowls — Criss' family called them "lifting dishes," and enormous platters heaped with fried potatoes and cured ham. We had a gallon pitcher that held milk from our own cow, and always a big bowl of yellow butter. Mom had a bread pan, the likes of which I have never seen before or after. It was so big it would barely fit in the oven, and she would bake it full of biscuits, plus a smaller pan. We usually ate all of them. I would like to see all the biscuits that she has baked in her lifetime piled in a heap. I saw her buy a little cardboard tube of canned biscuits the other day, and it was a shock. The old table is gone, the bench with its row of grubby young'ens is gone, and Mom eats alone.

The Clay Free Press
January 27, 1982

Our last snowfall was truly spectacular. Even those who are thoroughly sick and tired of snow had to agree. It came early in the morning as a fine mist, but by midmorning, large, fluffy flakes were floating down on hill and valley. Soon rooftop, hillside and road were covered by a thick blanket of white. It was a soft, clinging snow that hung on every twig and branch. The next morning the sun came out on a fairyland of ice and snow. Every bit of ugliness, from roadside litter to tumbledown shack, was covered with a mantle of pure white. The lowliest bush by the wayside was decked out in cotton candy perfection. The pine trees drooped down under their burden, and the red berries on the holly bush peeped shyly through their frosting of white. But as one kid remarked, "That first snow was thrilling, but now I'd like to see some bare ground."

The good Lord must have known what we needed and sent a couple of mild days. With their rich promise of spring, it has been a boon to our spirits and a blessing to our souls. Next week might bring more cold and snow, but we have the assurance that spring will come. The crocuses have poked their brave little heads up through the thawing soil, and deep underground, other spring flowers, almost ready to thrust a tentative finger toward the warming sun, are stretching and stirring.

February has always been the month that we dig sassafras. You have to dig it when the ground thaws out enough to get a mattock down through it, and yet before the sap goes up in the trunk of the tree.

The big roots have the most robust flavor, turning a deep red when brewed long enough. This is really a mountain drink, and to me the most delicious one discovered. Sassafras tea is supposed to be a good spring tonic, and we all look forward to it. You can peel the fragrant bark from the root, dry it, and keep it for two or three years. We usually just chunk up the whole root, cover it with water, and boil it over and over again.

A lover's moon hangs in the February sky tonight — its round fullness gleaming on the frost-covered ground. It seems suspended above Pilot Knob, mysterious and glowing with a bright yellow luminescence that is reflected in the running water of the creek. It seems fitting that a full moon should usher in Valentine's Day, which is just around the corner.

I guess I am sentimental, but I have cards the kids made me back through the years. With their uneven lettering and unusual prose, they bring a warm glow to my heart. One from Andy had this verse, "I know you are tired, and don't like to work, but you keep on working, and never stop." Sometimes I wonder what kind of an impression I made on my kids. Another one, not so original but extremely graphic, quoted, "Roses are red, violets are purple, sugar is sweat, and so's maple syrple. You are sweat, and so am I."

Back in the years, a young man named Ode was sweet on a certain girl and bought her a box of candy for Valentine's Day. He enlisted the help of my Uncle Enos and his friend Elmer to wrap and mail the candy to her. Uncle Enos reassured Ode that they would take care of the matter. Of course, you can guess the rest. They ate the bottom layer of candy, then carefully wrapped pieces of raw potato and put them back in the box. They dutifully wrapped and mailed the box to the girl. Sometime later Ode sadly told the boys, "I don't know what happened to her. She has never spoken to me since I sent her the candy!" I don't think they ever told him.

There is an old saying that it is a wise father who knows his own son, but sometimes it takes a wise mother to recognize him. We hadn't seen our oldest son's face for more thán three years, due to the growth of a full beard. I came into the living room to find Kevin and a strange young man talking to Criss. I started to ask Kevin who his friend was, when the young man looked me straight in the eye. He was vaguely familiar, and it dawned on me that it was my own son, Mike — sans beard. After whooping with laughter, I finally gasped, "Mike, you look just like me!" "I know," he said in disgust. "I'm gonna grow it back!"

The Clay Free Press
February 10, 1982

There is an old valentine in my box of yesterday's treasures. The red satin heart has faded to pink, and the fragrance is dry and dusty. Forty years ago it was inscribed, "Love forever."

His eyes were as clear and blue as the skies over the hills in springtime, and he was tall and straight as one of the poplars that grow on its wooded slopes. I don't know when love first dawned in my heart.

I'd known him since childhood — we were distant cousins and usually saw one another during the glorious fall season when all the world was aglow. His grandfather, with whom he lived, had settled deep in the hills; isolated from neighbors or civilization. My father always took our family on a camping trip during squirrel season, and we would camp in the woods near his home.

I can still smell the warm, brown, earthy fragrance that was unique to that place, compounded of rich earth, dry leaves, pine needles and warm sunshine. The rhododendrons and hemlocks grew right down to the edge of the narrow dirt road, and the creek was always clear and cold. It was a place of peace and quiet, set apart from the rush of the everyday world.

I guess we were teenagers when I first noticed him as a handsome boy, and not just a buddy romping with me in the woods and playing in the creek. That was a magical fall, with the awakening of love. Never did the woods gleam so radiantly, or the creek tumble by so clear and sparkling. He showed me where the deer berries ripened, tiny and red, creeping over the huge boulders that rose up out of the creek bed. He pointed out the silvery minnows that darted under and around the tumbled rocks in the creek, and we laughed and splashed in the cold water. He guided me through the rhododendron thickets and showed me the hidden places where the timid deer bedded down. He climbed trees that were entangled with wild grapevines and dropped the tiny black pods in my upraised hands. Those were sweet, innocent days that were soon gone . . .

Time passed, and like so many of our sturdy mountaineer boys, he volunteered to serve his country as a soldier. He was only seventeen when he enlisted — just a green country boy fresh from the hills of Clay County. The army soon took care of his greenness. It also finished his boyhood. A fine, handsome soldier he made, straight and tall in his uniform. Due a leave home at Christmas, he was bitterly disappointed when he spent the holidays in a base hospital. After eight weeks of basic training, he had come down with pneumonia. He was miserably homesick, but the Army put him through several more weeks of infantry combat training before he got a short leave home. We had written many letters, and love had grown. He kissed me then for the first time, and there were stars in my eyes as we made plans for the future.

The address on his letters changed suddenly to San Francisco. He had been shipped out. The next one came from Japan — but he was moving on. Then they came from places with strange names — Koje-do, (where he spent his eighteenth birthday), Pusan, Tangangie.

He was lonely, and sometimes scared, and terribly homesick. He missed his family and the familiar things of home. He wrote wistful letters, remembering the simple things of boyhood. He longed for the farm where he was raised: for the deer and the squirrel. There would be no deer or squirrel hunting for him that fall.

In February he wrote that he would be home before the leaves turned again. He talked about the hills of Korea, but they were nothing like ours. In April he wrote, "The flowers are blooming here now. They're beautiful. They remind me of home. I get sort of a lost feeling when I see where everything has been torn up by shells and bombs. I guess it can't be helped, but it seems such a shame that things so beautiful as flowers and trees should be destroyed, and all because of a silly war. I thought I knew what it was all about when I first came over here, but now I'm beginning to wonder. I have been overseas for almost a year, and I hope you won't think I am feeling sorry for myself. I am proud to have done what little I could to help. I know that I am no better than many others who have fought and even died over here. But is it worth it? Sometimes I wonder . . . "

The next letter was dated May 27. He was so excited, and asked me not to write anymore. In fifteen days, he would be on his way home! He wrote, "It has been a long, rough road but it's almost over now. P.S. I made another stripe today."

I got the letter three days after the telegram came from the War Department telling us he had been killed in action during a volunteer patrol mission. He was eighteen years and ten months old. He did come home before the leaves turned. As the last silvery note of "Taps" echoed from the hollow below, his body was laid to rest on a hillside deep in his beloved woods.

I know that the deer berries still grow on the boulders above the creek, and the deer still bed down in the secret, hidden places. The silver minnows dart in and out in the creek, and the tangy wild grapes ripen in the tree tops.

I don't go there any more.

The Charleston Gazette, February 14, 1991
The Clay Herald, February 11, 1992

Yesterday's spring-like weather has fled before the gray drizzle that today has brought. The yard looks bare and forlorn with all the snow gone; winter's debris can be seen clearly. The occasional sunbeam reveals windows streaked with the grime that a hard winter has left behind. It is the dingiest time of the year when everything looks tired and winter-weary.

There are unmistakable signs of spring that point to warmer weather ahead. The pointed heads of the daffodils stand bravely in this rain that has now turned to snow. It won't be long, though, until the spring calves will begin appearing.

I dug an old coat out of the closet on the back porch (a hand-me-down from Aunt May, with a genuine mink collar) and to my dismay, I found the fur chewed up and half gone. I had to smile at the thought of baby mice, pink and hairless, nestled in their sumptuous bed of mink. I thought about Oscar, Ronnie's pet mouse that he had when he was a youngster. He rescued him from certain death when he was only a few days old, after Daddy had uncovered a mice nest in the barn. Oscar thrived, with care and devotion from Ronnie, to a fine state of young mousehood, sleek and gray. One day he made the mistake of sinking his sharp teeth in Ronnie's finger, and the blood squirted. Oscar met an untimely end, for which I am sure Daddy was thankful.

Our children had hamsters for a period of time, and they were almost as bad as field mice. It finally came to the place where Criss issued an ultimatum — it was either the hamsters or him. The kids all voted to keep the hamsters, but I counted my vote worth three of theirs, and the hamsters went.

The Clay Free Press
February 14, 1982

March has flung a few mild, sunny days our way and departed in a swirl of snowy skirts, with trailing icicles in her hair. The creek that was locked in solid ice for a week is now flowing smoothly down to Big Laurel Creek and on to Elk River. The ice is breaking up in the river in huge, grinding chunks.

It is too early to start spring cleaning, but I'll never be accused of being a good housekeeper anyway. Criss was lying on the couch commenting on my cobwebs. "A man has no business lying on the couch looking at cobwebs," I told him furiously. I think they make a place look homey.

I'm afraid I'm going to have to shape up — Matthew has begun courting, and he is a different person. He even wants his clothes ironed! I gave my ironing board away years ago, and hid the iron. Why not? Sometimes when I would finally get around to the ironing basket, I would discover that the children had outgrown their clothes months ago. I would pass them on down to the younger cousins and think smugly, "Let their mothers iron them." Matthew has turned from a kid that didn't know how to pick up a wet towel from the bathroom floor to a cleaning fanatic who hides the trash can and covers the torn places in the vinyl armchair with shoe polish. "What if she came to visit?" he moans. "Why don't we get some new furniture and put some vinyl siding on the house?" (In the middle of winter?) I have heard a litany of her family's virtues for months. Their home is lovely, refined and charming. Her dad looks like Tom Selleck, and her mother is young and beautiful. "She looks like Tammy, only older." (Tammy is a beauty contest winner.) How can I, in my middle-aged fatness, compete with that? Even their cat is sleek and handsome. Our part Persian kitten, Sybil, looks distinctly uncomfortable and tries to smooth down her ratty fur with an apologetic tongue. I know just how she feels. Criss and I went on a successful diet last week. He lost seven pounds, and I gained five. Well, somebody had to eat all the food he left.

I just got the word — SHE will probably come to visit next week. I could make her some soup and show her my cobwebs. That should impress her.

My sister Susie reports that her children are going through the same self-conscious stage where they are embarrassed by everything their mother does. Well, join the club. They do eventually outgrow this,

I think. Matthew used to hide under the dashboard of the truck when he and his father had to transport a load of trash through Clay on their way to the city dump. Now he will take the truck by himself for this chore. We are still not allowed to use words in front of Tammy such as "trash" "dump" "garbage" or any other of the mundane words pertaining to daily living. She called the other day and Criss innocently told her that Matthew had gone to the dump. He was highly incensed when he returned. Susie said Criss should have told her that Matthew was on an environmental clean-up detail. Live and learn.

Your own children can be turned so differently. Patty and I watched Crystal catch the bus this morning, her coat slung over one arm. (It was fifteen degrees out.) I made her take the coat, but she wouldn't put it on. She was mincing delicately in toeless flats across the expanse of ice and snow. Patty stated, "Look at that — if that were me back in high school, I'd be wearing three pairs of knee socks and a pair of combat boots." She would have, too. She romped through four years of high school and didn't care about impressing anyone.

A lot of people bewail the fact that their children grow up and leave the nest. I enjoyed my children while they were home, but I also enjoy the ones who have reached adulthood and are on their own. Your children can be your friends as well as your offspring, and are a source of comfort as you grow older. I am thankful that I was raised in a big family, and that we have a big family of our own. We may have had to cut the cake in smaller pieces, but we always managed to make it go around.

The Clay Free Press
February 1, 1984

The lovely, sunny Sunday has ended, tucked neatly away by the shell-pink sunset that wrapped all the loose ends of the day and put them away for the night. This has been a day plucked right out of the middle of spring's bounty and presented to us in the midst of March's bleakness. The spring birds tried hard to awaken the sleeping leaves and flowers, but there was no response other than the shimmering patina of green on the meadow grass. I looked in vain for the shining gold of the coltsfoot, whose cheery blossoms are the first of the spring flowers. But the flowers and leaves slept wisely on, knowing that too soon an advent would invite frostbitten buds and frozen blossoms.

March is a thawing month, as the hand of winter relaxes its grip on the frozen land. Every year we look eagerly for spring, forgetting about the mud that comes first. Did you ever combine a warm, muddy day with seven little grandsons? Luke is the worst of the bunch — Patty calls him a dirt magnet. His Aunt Peggy took him to town one day and had to stop and buy a can of soda pop to clean him up with. That's almost as bad as having your face washed with a dishrag when Mom looked up to see unexpected company coming. The only thing that compared was having to sleep at the foot of the bed when all the cousins came to visit. I have experienced both. There are some things the younger generation have been spared — these joys of the good old days. (Luke was dirty again when they reached their destination.) I don't think I'd recognize him with a clean face. Sometimes when the girls divide their brood at nightfall, and the day's mud is washed off in the bathtub, I wonder if they end up with the right kids.

Patty said she opened the door yesterday and found Aaron and Luke standing there, both weeping as if their hearts would break. Luke's face was dirty as usual, with two clean streaks where the tears were coursing down. Alarmed, she asked, "What on earth is the matter with Luke?" "He's crying 'cause he wants to go to heaven," six-year-old Aaron replied between sobs. "Then why are you crying, Aaron?" she questioned further. He gulped, "I'm crying 'cause I don't want him to go!"

The boys are a handful, but I will put sister Susie's five-year-old Alison up against them any time. We were in the kitchen, and all at once we could hear the definite patter of little feet on the roof. We ran outside to investigate, to find Alison calmly walking around on the edge of the roof. Susie was scared almost speechless, and after she had tolled her down to the ground, she demanded angrily, "What on earth were you trying to do, Alison?" Alison looked surprised at all the fuss and patiently explained, "Why, I was just a bein' Wonder Woman!"

The Clay Free Press
February 15, 1984

Poor Sybil is dead; a victim of love (hers) and thoughtlessness (mine.) She was just a tiny scrap of fur when we got her from a Calhoun County farm. Her mother was a barn cat, and her father was just passing through. Somewhere there must have been a Persian ancestor that gave her a coat of abundant fur and a jaunty air of having seen better days. Having been raised all of her short life in a barn, she had a defensive air and a spitfire attitude about her that repelled our attempts to pet her. Patience won out, however, and in a few days she was running to our call and rubbing her head against our fingers.

She suffered the grandchildren to pet her, but

she was my property . . . or was I hers? When I would sit down in the swing on the porch, she would come running to hop up beside me and wait to be caressed. "Listen, Mommaw, her motor is running," Abigail told me. When I was busy, and she was hungry, she would tap me gently with a sheathed paw. If I still didn't notice her, she would tap again in a half-apologetic manner. She followed me like a dog; in fact, I think she watched the door for me to come out. When I went to the post office, she was right at my heels, and when I fed the chickens, she would go with me. That was her undoing.

It was almost dark when I took a walk to my sister Jeannies'. The air was balmy, and I felt the need for some exercise. I should have known that Sybil would tag along, but to tell the truth, I wasn't even thinking about her. It was a lovely walk in the spring-like air, and I relaxed and enjoyed the world about me. Hurrying home, I met a few cars in the semi-dark, but I never noticed a fuzzy little cat following in my footsteps.

Early the next morning, my daughter found her in the ditchline, a lifeless handful of fur with the life snuffed out. I hope she died instantly, with her last thought being that we were almost home. I miss her when I open the door early in the morning, and she is not there with her "cat smile" of good morning. It seems that I can hear the rustle of soft, padded feet behind me when I walk through the yard, but when I turn around it is only the echo of my own footsteps. Every time I lose a pet I dearly love, I vow that I will never get attached to an animal again. But I invariably do. A pet gives so much in return for so little. They love without qualification, and are loyal without reason. Our lives are enriched by them, even when we

love them, only to lose them.
The Clay Free Press
February 22, 1984

The last week of spring-like weather is over, and winter is with us still. While it lasted, it coaxed the tulip and iris bulbs through the ground and swelled the buds on the lilac bush. The spring birds are singing lustily, and my young pullets rejoiced in the warm sunlight. They scratched industriously in the warming earth, their tail feathers sticking up like ruffled petticoats. Every day they present me with a dozen or so fresh brown eggs. I have a special feeling for these chickens that I hatched late last summer from two settings of eggs. Someone called and asked about purchasing an old hen to make a pot of chicken and dumplings. I felt as if they had asked for one of the kids. I'm not about to murder my chickens. They are part of the family.

Snowflakes swirl and eddy around our Clay County hills once more, silencing the spring peepers that had begun their preliminary chorus of spring gladness. We are driven back in the house for a little longer to wait for warm weather.

The West Virginia countryside glows in the winter with a stark beauty. The trees lift graceful, bare branches to the sky and the sycamore's bleached-bone limbs shine with luminescent light. The brown of the hills form a perfect backdrop for the green of the pine trees, while the low-lying rhododendron bushes form dark masses along the hillsides. I love the rock formations which can be seen clearly now. Jutting out from the steep hillside, or silhouetted against the sky on the very crest of a hill, they stand solid and durable, unchanging as time goes by.

Sometimes when I am out in the woods, I think about the Indians who once roamed these hills, climbed over the same rocks, and now are gone and forgotten. In time, I too will be gone, but the rocks will still be here — enduring and immovable.

Last week as I drove up Elk River and looked at the outcroppings of rock on the steep hills above the river, I got a yearning to climb Buzzard Rock once again. Just about everyone in this vicinity has climbed Buzzard Rock at one time or another. I remember the first time Daddy took us to Buzzard Rock — I thought it must surely be the biggest rock in the whole world. We packed a picnic lunch that day, and along with Mom, all seven of us children, plus a horse named Topsy, set out for Buzzard Rock. It was a five or six-mile-trip uphill and through the woods to a very isolated section of the country. There it loomed, a huge rock right on the top of a hill, seeming too steep for any little girl to climb. But urged on and helped by Daddy, hands trembling and heart quaking, we made it to the top. A ceaseless wind blows on the top of that rock, and carved on the face of it must be the initials of everyone who has ever lived in or passed through Clay County. Proudly, Daddy showed us where he had carved his and Mom's initials right after they were married. We all added our initials, and spent a happy day there. Except for me — I was in mortal terror that one of the kids would fall off the rock.

Daddy showed us the stone steps that had been cut out at the base of the rock which had once led into a cave. The opening had fallen in. As boys, Daddy and his friends had explored there as deep as they dared to go, and one of the boys had left a shucking peg on the last step to show how far they had gone.

We had much excited conjecture as to who had made the steps and why. We surmised that the Indians must have used the rock for some purpose. It never occurred to us what earthly use they would have for a large rock in the middle of nowhere. Our heads were always stuffed with many notions anyway. One time we decided that there must be an Indian burial mound in the middle of Mom's chicken lot. We dug the whole summer long, and all we ever found for our pains were some chicken bones and a few broken pieces of Mom's Blue Willow ware — plus a big hole that you could bury a cow in.

They tell me that Buzzard Rock looks different now. The oil company has made a road to it, and you can easily walk to the top of it without having to scale its steep sides. I'm sure it doesn't look as big and forbidding as it did when I was little. Perhaps I won't go back — it might spoil the memory.

The Clay Free Press
February 9, 1983

The early frogs have already begun their mating song up in the pond. These are the ones that sound like a flock of strangled ducks, and it would certainly take another frog to appreciate that melody. What warms my heart are the spring peepers that send out a shrill, piping song from every marsh and pond. I feel that they are the true harbingers of spring.

When the March wind dried up the mud at Hagar School, it was the signal for the marble games to begin. Bicycles were rare, and skateboards non-existent, but everyone had marbles. The old two-room school house had a large playground, completely devoid of grass, and tromped smooth by hundreds of running feet. It made an ideal place to play marbles. (It was good for hopscotch, too — all you needed was a piece or two of broken glass or some pebbles, and perfect balance.) The girls played hopscotch; no boy would be caught dead playing such a sissy game. But we girls were not above playing marbles — with each other, of course. With our knobby knees grinding in the dirt, and our pigtails sticking straight out, we played "Four Holes and a Peewee" with much squealing and giggling.

The boys played with deadly aim and deadly earnestness. With shouts of "I got dibs on you," and "No fudgin'" to "Knucks down," they played their ring marble games every recess and at noon hour. Each boy had his favorite shooting marble, called a "kimmy" or a "shooter," which he guarded well. Daddy never allowed us to play "Keeps," considering it a form of gambling, but my husband's family must not have had such qualms. When we got married, Criss had a small churn full of marbles. Time, sons, and grandsons have well disposed of them.

Mothers must surely look back on our marble games with mixed emotions because they took their toll in the knees of our overall pants. It was impossible to keep the holes out. Mom patched the patches and the games went on . . .

It has been years since I've seen little boys down on their knees playing marbles. Sometimes I get the urge to gather up the grandsons and teach them to play the old marble games that we loved.

When the marble games began, winter was over.

The Clay Free Press
March 2, 1983

We have walked in these hills, through the years

and in many seasons together. Which is the best season? Early spring of course, says the little child, when all the world is born anew. It is so good to know the security of a happy home; the contentment of having every need supplied by a mother and a father. Not so, says the teenage girl. It must be late spring, when all the birds are bursting with song, and the flowers blossom in every corner. That is the time of awakening love and blossoming womanhood. The young mother smiles and declares that midsummer is surely the best season. With her little ones around her, innocent and trusting, she looks at the lush growth of summer, its green and growing season. No, it's the early autumn, avows the matron whose children are leaving the nest. There is a slowing down of nature; the growing season is over and the most beautiful time of the year is here. She basks in the changing autumn colors, and thinks of the leisure time she now has for herself.

It is mid autumn for me, and it is the best time of my life. I enjoy so this stage, rich in grandchildren and full of contentment. There is time for hobbies now in the golden days of retirement. Autumn has always been my favorite season, after the crops are gathered and the gold of autumn is sprinkled over the hills.

I know that winter lies ahead, that white season of long sleep for the earth. But why should I fear, when the same Lord who has led me through all the other seasons will lead me through the last one? It may be an unknown place to me, but He has walked the way before me and will guide my steps. Just as He gently lulls the flowers to sleep in the fall, to put forth buds and bloom afresh in another spring, so will He take care of me.

I am confident that the best is yet to be.

THE END